PRAYER
IN THE
SECULAR
CITY

PRAYER
IN THE
SECULAR CITY

by

DOUGLAS RHYMES

LUTTERWORTH PRESS
LONDON

First published 1967
Second impression 1969
Third impression 1971

Lutterworth Press
4 *Bouverie Street, London, E.C.*4

ISBN 0 7188 0772 3

Printed in Great Britain
by
The Bowering Press, Plymouth

To
the eight Junior Clergy of the
Southwark Diocese
who have helped me greatly in my thinking:

JOHN AUSTIN, CHRISTOPHER BROWN, NORMAN DAVIES, MARTIN HUGHES, PAUL JOBSON, DAVID LAMBOURNE, ROGER ROYLE, and DAVID WILSON.

ACKNOWLEDGMENTS

In a work such as this the author has had inevitably to draw on a number of sources for examples and illustrations. He would wish to express his gratitude for the help thus afforded, and in particular for permission to make rather extensive quotations from the following:

Honest to God, by J. A. T. Robinson, Bishop of Woolwich, published by S.C.M. Press, Ltd.

Le Milieu Divin, by Teilhard de Chardin, published by Collins, Sons & Co. Ltd.

Modern Psalms by Boys, compiled by Raymond Hearn, published by the University of London Press, Ltd.

Only One Way Left, by George MacLeod, published by the Iona Community.

Prayers of Life, by Michael Quoist, published by Gill & Son Ltd., Dublin

Thought, from the *Complete Poems* of D. H. Lawrence, published by Heinemann Ltd., and quoted by permission of Laurence Pollinger Ltd. and the estate of the late Mrs. Frieda Lawrence.

Eleanor Rigby, from *Revolver*, Copyright (©) by Northern Songs Ltd., words and music by John Lennon and Paul McCartney.

He is also grateful for permission to print experimental services included in Appendix 2 and Appendix 3.

CONTENTS

CHAPTER I

INTRODUCTION: THE MODERN MALAISE IN PRAYER

Some years ago Bonhoeffer asked the question: "What is the place of prayer and worship in the entire absence of religion?" That is the question which fills the minds of many in the secularized world of to-day. It is a question which in a slightly different form is being asked not only outside the Church but also by many within. The way in which they put the question is: "What does prayer mean today?" "What am I doing when I am praying?" "What pattern of prayer makes sense and relevance in the kind of world in which I live?" "Teach me to pray in the way that man of the twentieth century can with meaning pray."

Evidence is forthcoming from all sides that the demand for a relevant spirituality is being made with ever greater insistence and with something approaching despair from both clergy and laity. A group of laity meeting at a Bristol Conference about two years ago said: "Teach us a pattern of lay spirituality, not clergy spirituality or monastic spirituality, but lay spirituality in the world today."

At weekend after weekend at the Southwark Diocesan Training Centre, when lay people come together there is revealed the barrenness of their prayer life. They complain that when they kneel to pray at the end of the day nothing happens save a vacuum, and they are going on doing this without any real expectation, as an intolerable burden, a duty painfully to be borne without any feeling that what they are doing constitutes any source of strength for meeting the problems and anxieties of their secular life. They complain bitterly that either they receive no teaching from the clergy about prayer after Confirmation instruction, or that the teaching is couched in the familiar and routine patterns of Confession, Thanksgiving, Intercession and Petition which have become meaningless to them. They dimly suspect either that the clergy know all about it and are in a privileged position, or that the clergy do not themselves attach the importance they profess to this life of prayer.

If this is true of the laity, the same barrenness and malaise about prayer are equally true of the clergy. Many of the traditional forms of spirituality have gone dead on them. At a recent conference of junior clergy it became clear that many had given up saying the Offices as having no meaning for them, that in many parishes there was no common meeting of the staff for Offices or for Meditation, and practically no young curate had ever had discussion with his vicar about his spiritual life, nor did such discussion ever seem to be contemplated as a necessity of a communal clergy life.

Recently I met eight young clergymen from very different kinds of tradition to discuss with them what kind of training should be taking place in the final year at theological college: they were unanimous in their complaints about what they called the "imposed" patterns of spirituality they encountered at college, and one of the recommendations most strongly made was that whatever was done in the way of corporate prayer or worship at college should be worked out by students and staff asking together the questions: "What do we mean by prayer? What do we mean by worship?" and only after such discussion should any common pattern be evolved. At a Prayer Workshop Conference at Maidstone the report read:

> Most of the group find little meaning in prayer when it is thought of as talking to God, or listening to God, or tuning in to God. The metaphor of dialogue does not mean very much. None of our attempts at defining prayer meant very much (in the sense of having any significance for us): "A way of getting into contact with God" or "Prayer helps to enter into the mystery of life" or "Prayer is aligning our wills with the will of Christ."

Sufficient will have been said to indicate that this is a major problem of today for both clergy and laity. The first question, then, that we must ask if we would hope to find answers to this problem is: are there special factors in the world of today which have a particular bearing upon these difficulties, which accentuate the normal difficulties of prayer and make it likely that this age would find it more difficult to know how to pray?

I think there are three fundamental reasons which contribute directly to the present difficulties. The first is the kind of age in which we live, its characteristics, and its ethos, which for various reasons, into which I will go, strongly militate against considering prayer as a factor in altering events, and also make the kind of concentration that goes with prayer increasingly difficult. The second is the confusion of the current debate about God. Prayer and faith are inseparable, and obviously the belief about the meaning of the word God will profoundly affect the prayer which is addressed to God, and much of present-day theological thinking would make a definition of prayer as "talking to God" impossible. The third difficulty is the limitations which we have put upon the word "prayer" for ourselves as constituting a special kind of activity at special times and in special places; we have to ask ourselves the question: is the word "prayer" thus restricted, or is there a wider view of prayer which can speak more to the understanding of life in this present age?

Let me now examine each one of these in greater detail, for such examination will help not only to see the difficulties but also perhaps give some of the clues to the ways by which these difficulties must be met.

CHAPTER 2

THE BACKGROUND OF MODERN PRAYER: THE CHARACTERISTICS OF THIS AGE

(a) *A Society with no Explicit Philosophy or Sense of Meaning*

A secular society as has been demonstrated for us in both Harvey Cox's *Secular City* and D. L. Munby's *Idea of a Secular Society* is a society which has no official aims or purposes, no stated or explicit philosophy. It is a neutral society in which no one governs by divine right and no group's ideas are accepted as having any authority for the whole. Within our present society it matters little to anyone what religious views are held: it is a tolerant society, and therefore one may belong to any Church or none, and no one will officially worry at all. There is no longer any kind of ontological system to which most men subscribe: there is now an openness which has turned away from the metaphysical thinking of the past in which men's understanding of truth was in relation to some kind of ontological totality from which all truth flowed: "Theology, the queen of sciences". As Harvey Cox says:

> Two motifs characterize the style of the secular city . . . pragmatism and profanity. By pragmatism we mean secular man's concern with the question "will it work". The world is viewed not as a unified metaphysical system but as a series of problems and projects. By profanity we refer to man's wholly terrestrial horizon, the disappearance of any supramundane reality defining his life . . . he views the world not in terms of some other world but in terms of itself (*The Secular City*, pp. 60 and 61).

It will be obvious that such an outlook produces great problems for concepts of prayer, for modern man will not look for the solution of his problems to the attempts to influence a being of another world to be concerned with them, nor will he expect the divine intervention of a God to be the effectual means of dealing with disease and war. Rather will he see problems as needing the skill of increasingly specialist knowledge, and, where these problems are not solvable at present, he will simply expect them to be solved as knowledge increases and more technical attention is paid to them in all fields of research. The answer to man's pain lies in the field of medical research; the answer to men's needs lies in the right use of nuclear and economic research; the answer to man's sense of guilt lies in psychological analysis. It is not surprising that in this kind of atmosphere scant attention will be paid to prayer.

In the same way, this is not only a profane age, it is also a pragmatic age: the way in which man looks at every question is to ask: "Does it work?" "Does it function?" "Is it relevant?" I recently had an interesting experience of this when I had to address three different groups of people on three successive nights: the first a University Humanist Society, the second a College of Technology, and the third a group of high-powered consultant psychiatrists. None of these groups were Christian groups but the questions they asked about Christianity revealed an entirely pragmatic outlook: "What difference is there between a Christian and non-Christian in the ordinary everyday world of work, neighbourhood and personal relationships?" "What kind of different values, different attitudes, different relationships does the Christian bring to life?" "What is the point of prayer and worship—what difference does it make to the world of everyday living?" Spirituality will only make sense in present-day society if it is seen to work and to relate to the world in which we live. As the Bishop of Woolwich says in *The New Reformation*:

> Men of our age trained in a scientific empirical discipline are requiring again to see before they can believe.

There is a very great deal of difference between the patterns of thought of the mediaeval ages and of our age about the effect of prayer on the world. Van Buren points out in *The Secular Meaning of the Gospel*:

> When ancient man prayed that God send rain on his neighbour's fields he thought that he was doing the most effective thing he could in his exercise of his perspective as a Christian. Called to freedom for his neighbour he set out to help him. The best help he knew was God and his neighbour needed rain so that to help was to pray for rain, that was the use and the meaning of his prayer.

It is interesting to see that Van Buren, whose book carried to its most logical conclusion the present radical secularist thinking on religion, could also find no room for prayer as it would be normally understood. Prayer to him becomes no more than reflection and consequent action within a given situation. If one simply accepts current secularist thinking, there is no place for prayer within such thinking, but I believe, and shall endeavour to show, that there is no need to jettison prayer, but rather to heed the empirical and pragmatic demands of modern man in a spirituality which is seen to work and to relate to deeper understanding of *this* world rather than *some other* world.

(b) *The Existentialist Outlook of Modern Man*

Another important factor which very much influences current thinking about prayer and about God is the existentialist bias of most modern thinking. Existentialism, perhaps the most characteristic modern philosophy, is concerned to ask questions about the essential being of man: what is the existence which belongs to man in his concrete living, acting and deciding, what does human existence mean in the present age? These are questions which are naturally asked in a world overshadowed by the threat of no future in possible annihilation and in which change has been so rapid that the past almost seems to disappear as an element in the present. The modern generation, especially the younger generation, is passionately interested in the immediate present, in man himself, in the personal relationships of man, and, although probably many people would not frame their thinking consciously in terms of existentialist philosophy, it is nevertheless the question of what is authentic existence in the kind of world in which we now live which most concerns them.

How does all this thinking affect our view of prayer? Primarily in two ways. The first is that prayer must have something to say concerning the meaning of the present moment in relation to the ultimate meaning or reality behind all things if it is to speak to that aspect of existential thinking which is asking the questions of the meaningfulness of human existence, in which case we shall be thinking, not so much of prayer as talking to someone outside present existence, but rather of prayer as the reflections we make upon present existence in relation to what is truly authentic existence. Prayer will speak to that kind of living which is laying itself open to the reality or meaning of all living. The pattern of prayer here most akin to existentialist ways of thinking is nearly allied to the mystical thinking of Meister Eckhart and the Zen Buddhists. Secondly, prayer will have to speak to what Camus calls "tasting fully the passing moment". The holiness which will make the most sense to the modern generation of young people is the holiness which is neither concerned overmuch with the traditional patterns of the past nor built into visions of the future, whether they be of heaven or of earthly Utopias. The spirituality which will ring true will not be concerned with future happiness or past ontology but with the blessings of the present moment.

(c) *A Society of Much Noise, Many Contacts and Considerable Mobility*

Other factors in modern society which make prayer difficult are the increase and the necessity of noise to many people, the restless activity of modern life, and the increasing mobility with its lack of roots in society.

To take them in order, let us first mention the increase of noise. Not only is noise the normal background of most modern living but to many, especially young people, it has become a necessity to have this background. Many young people of my acquaintance find it impossible to work without a background of pop music. (One young man I know did a complicated Ph.D. thesis to the entire accompaniment of this music—nothing short of a miracle to me but he needed this to *aid* not to *hinder* his concentration!) One has only to visit the youth club, the normal home, the beach where young people gather, to see how absolutely necessary to life has become quite deafening noise making conversation impossible.

But if this is so, how do we square this with that need of quiet, which has always been the background of meditation or contemplation, with the Retreat in which it is assumed that the silence aids concentration, on the theory of "Be still and know that I am God"? Does this mean that the modern generation are going to find it increasingly difficult to pray because prayer demands quiet, or does it mean that we have to give up thinking that for many people prayer demands quiet and so provide a background of concentration; that the modern Retreat for young people would not be a house of silence, but a house filled with loud pop-music in which with this background it would be possible for them to concentrate their thoughts on God as the young man I have mentioned concentrated on his Ph.D. thesis!

We have also the pressures of time. We live in a generation who have become the slaves of time. We are often no longer in control of time, but time is in control of us; we, as one wag put it, are constantly arriving late at one meeting and leaving early in order that we may arrive late at the next! We often say that we have no time for prayer and no time for worship, and this is for many a sheer statement of fact; maybe they ought to make time, but one knows that such is the pressure of life that it will be a counsel of perfection to talk to them in terms of setting aside so many minutes or hours each day for prayer. Michel Quoist has caught this aspect of modern life well in one of his prayers when he says:

> And so all men run after time, Lord.
> They pass through life running—hurried, jostled, overburdened, frantic
> and they never get there. They haven't time.
> In spite of all their efforts they're still short of time, of a great deal of time.
> Lord, you must have made a mistake in your calculation.
> There is a big mistake somewhere.
> The hours are too short,
> The days are too short,
> Our lives are too short. (*Prayers of Life*, p. 77.)

This lack of depth in life and sheer restlessness of life have even affected the life of most of our Churches. Many Churches these days are places of restless activity, over-organized, with a few people rushing to and fro propping up the organizations, a few priests rushing in and out of the organizations—all involved in a grand charade of busyness, so that it is rare, in Anglican Churches at least, to find anyone spending any time in them for reflective thought, whether he be priest or layman.

Listen to Evelyn Underhill on this:

> A shallow religiousness, the tendency to be content with a bright ethical piety wrongly called practical Christianity . . . seems to be one of the defects of institutional religion at the present time . . . and that is a type of religion which does not wear well. It does little for the soul in those awful moments when the pain and mystery of life are most deeply felt. (*Anthology of the Love of God*, p. 123.)

The sheer mobility of life will also affect prayer and tend to give a new slant to thinking about prayer. We live in an age when men are much less likely than ever before to settle down in any one place for any length of time. While this can be frustrating and has been deplored in many religious and romantic circles, it is not, as Harvey Cox has pointed out, without its advantages, for:

> Mobility is closely linked with social change: so guardians of the status quo have always opposed mobility. . . . Mobility in one area signified mobility in another. People on the move spatially are usually on the move intellectually, financially, psychologically. (*The Secular City*, pp. 52, 53)

This means that as far as spirituality is concerned there can be mobility here also: as men live less in fixed surroundings so they will become less fixed in their liturgical ideas if they are already worshippers, and freedom of liturgical experiment will gradually meet with less opposition, while for those outside the Church there will be much greater opportunity of interesting them in an atmosphere of change in thought about theology, worship or prayer.

(d) *A Society Needing Community and Understanding of Relationships*

The last factor of modern society which I would count important in its effect upon spirituality is the increase of loneliness which an increasingly mobile society brings. There is a realization of the importance of relationships at all levels, together with the understanding that there are different types of relationship appropriate to differing situations, e.g. the relationships appropriate to work or to neighbourhood are not of the same kind as those appropriate to more intimate family and personal relationships.

There seem at the moment to be two contradictory forces at work in the sphere of human relationships: the one towards an increasing anonymity and privacy, reflected in the way in which many modern blocks of flats are designed (without the communal courts of the old blocks and with everything contributing to the kind of existence in which no one need know his next-door neighbour); this leads to a drawing away from extensive relationships and an increasing concentration on intensive and intimate relationships. The other leads in the opposite direction—towards an increasing recognition of human loneliness and a seeking in small groups to find that community which is lacking in the ordinary world (hence the great increase in and need for group therapy methods in modern psychology and the moving towards group working in Church life). The lack of community in the large community leads to a groping after the finding of this in the small group. Eric James, in an article on *Towards a Relevant Spirituality*, notes this fact with importance for its bearing upon new patterns of spirituality:

> In every age God seems to have given a new gift of "religious community" appropriate to that age. It could well be that the small group or "cell" is God's gift to our age—something like the Servants of Christ the King in which there is fellowship that supports and sustains commitment, and the acceptance which encourages honesty, informality and flexibility.

This means that both these factors will affect contemporary thinking about spirituality: the tendency towards increasing intensity of individual personal relationships will mean that great stress will be put upon experience as a test of validity: what is real in human experience, rather than what is given from above, will be the test both for moral and for spiritual living. The test which Harry Williams advances for his thinking in the preface of *The True Wilderness*, namely, "I had decided that I would try to ask myself how far and in what way a doctrine or creed had become part of what I am . . . unless what I had to say came from the depths of my experience I was struck dumb" will also be the test of spirituality; in other words, the prayer and worship which will make sense today will be that which has become part of my experience of life, of what life is in depth and what I am when I look deep into myself. Equally, the tendency to look for community in small groups will mean that much of our spirituality will arise from group thinking; both forms of prayer and forms of worship will only ring true if they have arisen from the direct thinking of the group and are an expression of the life of the group.

These, then, are the particular characteristics of the modern age, which will not only make prayer difficult but will also show the way towards a relevant spirituality which can speak to this age. To sum up, it will be a spirituality which can be seen to work, to appeal to the pragmatic in man concerned with both the meaning of life and the effect of that meaning upon the day-to-day life of the world; it will be constantly asking questions about the existence of man and the meaning of authentic existence in the world of today, and it will be relating that authentic existence to both what is ultimately real and true and what is expressing that ultimate truth in the present moment; it will speak to the blessings of the present moment; it will accept the sociological circumstances of lack of quiet, of increasing pressure, and be seeking effective methods of concentration which take into account those factors and do not either ignore them or fly flat contrary to them; it will take into account the freedom to experiment in a mobility of forms of prayer and worship which a new mobility of living makes more possible: it will be concerned with what is at the heart of personal experience and be flexible in relation to personal experience and what is valid for each individual; and it will take note of the fact that the community life and understanding of small groups will produce their own forms of spirituality relevant to and expressive of the life of those groups.

CHAPTER 3

THE BACKGROUND OF MODERN PRAYER: THE DEBATE ABOUT GOD

We must now turn our attention to the effects upon traditional concepts of prayer of the current debate about the meaning of the term "God". Broadly speaking, this debate turns upon whether we speak of God as *a* being, or as Being itself: whether we speak of God as *a* person or think of the nature of being as personal. Quite obviously, this will make a great difference to the way we think about prayer: we can speak of talking to God if God is a being, or a person; it is very difficult to see how we can speak in any realistic sense of prayer as talking to God if we think of God as being, as ultimate reality, for how can you talk to being, to ultimate reality, to the personal rather than to a person? Whatever form the understanding may have been of the God "out there", whether crude or spiritual, nevertheless the popular conception of God has been of *a* Being somehow separated from the rest of beings heavenly or created, a Person existing in His own right as a separate and independent entity.

Traditional theology has argued from what we know exists—the world—to a Being beyond it, to the necessity of His existence as separate from the world and yet creator of the world. As the Bishop of Woolwich says in *Honest to God*:

> Everyone of us lives with some mental picture of God "out there", a God who exists above and beyond the world He has made, a God to whom we pray and to whom we go when we die—a self-subsistent divine being.

Now this has made the traditional concept of prayer reasonably easy to follow, even if somewhat anthropomorphic in application. Prayer has been taught as talking to God, and to talk to God means that I, a human being, address another Being out there and apart from me but nevertheless interested in and concerned with me, who will listen to what I say and will speak to me so that if I listen hard enough I can hear what He is telling me. So prayer has been taught as very like a human conversation except that you cannot see the person, and it appears to be normally a rather one-sided conversation. Perhaps writing a letter conveys the analogy, since then I am conveying my thoughts definitely to someone out there whom I believe to exist and with whom as a separate being I can have communication.

Nevertheless, even the traditional view of prayer as talking to a person does not really solve the difficulties about conceiving prayer as conversation with God. First, when I try to visualize the divine person to whom I am talking, I usually fall back on the picture conveyed to my mind by the earthly life of Jesus Christ; I form an image of the Christ as revealed in the Gospels and I hold that image before me. I find that the person I am addressing, although I call Him God, is in fact the person who can only be made real to me in ordinary human terms, who must be represented either by my imagination dwelling on that human life, or by pictures, or by crucifixes or other visual aids which help to plant firmly before me the Word made flesh. Any other way of understanding the God out there to whom I pray becomes impossible for me, and so what I am really having is often a human dialogue between myself and the picture formed by me and for me of the human Christ.

Even by the traditional view of prayer we find ourselves up against an imagery which is anthropomorphic, a language which is not shared, a feeling about the converse which makes it very different from any converse we know, and certain grave difficulties about the communication of God's side of the talking since in very few cases does it seem obvious to the pray-er what God is trying to say to him.

It would seem, then, that the definition of prayer as talking to God lays itself open to some very serious difficulties, even by the traditional lines of thinking about God as a person, and it is by no means possible to teach prayer, as some clergy seem to have tried, as a simple comparison between talking to human beings and talking to God.

If, however, the difficulties of treating prayer in this way are great when thinking of God in traditional terms, they become even greater if we accept, as many do, the way of thinking about God which is characteristic of modern radical theology. For modern thinking has cast grave doubts on the possibility of the concept of God as a separate person, whether there is any more a God out there spiritually than a God out there literally and physically. This, the radical thinkers say, detracts from the uniqueness of God and simply places him in the categories of separateness from human life but alongside human life. In the thinking of Tillich, the main argument against the notion of God as a separate being is that it transforms the infinity of God into a finiteness which is merely an extension of the categories of finitude and places a divine world alongside but separated from the human world. This easily leads, as it has led, especially in Protestant theology, into a separation of the sacred from the secular, and has caused the practice of religion to be looked upon as a departmental activity existing alongside other activities.

It is also argued that the systematization of God is simply part of a particular philosophical system, the working out of the notions of supreme being in Greek philosophy which belong to the mediaeval city state, and that to define God in terms of dogma which can be accepted on authority is to impose upon him our love of order and systematization. As A. Vidler says:

> To insist that God shall be defined in terms that we can comprehend is to be like the children of Israel who refused to be satisfied with the eternal, invisible God that Moses and the Prophets proclaimed to them and who insisted on erecting idols of wood and stone which they could see with their eyes and touch with their hands. Any definition of God that purported to be at all adequate would be an idol of the mind. (*Christian Belief*, pp. 16, 17)

However, it is not my province within the scope of this book to argue exhaustively the case for the radical view of God, but simply to say that increasingly many are finding this view of

God satisfactory to their thinking, having much more to say to the modern empirical and existential mood. On the whole, it is this group both among clergy and laity who are seeking to see what this view of God has to say to their own thinking about prayer and what prayer means by this concept of God.

Personality is in no way confined to thinking of God as a sort of super-person somewhere "out there", but rather it is the nature of that ultimate reality which is God which we understand through our own experience of the purest kind of personal relationships. Like many other things it is rather understood through living than through definition, through the act of commitment which is the true nature of faith—namely the act of commitment which will experience the truth of its beliefs only when the commitment has been made. This is very finely brought out in a remarkable novel called *Incognito* by Petru Dumitriu when, after all his experiences of brutality and cruelty through, at first, war, and then in Communist concentration camps, he arrives at an understanding of what has been happening to him in the following terms:

> That was it: the sense and meaning of the universe was love; that was where all the turns of my life had been leading me. Why had I expected the world to justify itself to me and prove its meaning? It was for me to justify the world by loving it and forgiving it, to discover its meaning through love, to reveal it through forgiveness.

In other words, it is when we begin to exercise love that we begin to understand the nature of God, the meaning of the universe, for our act of faith that personal love is at the heart of all things brings the knowledge that this is so by the practice of it in the realm of the here and now life. As we will see later on, this has great implications for our thinking about prayer, for the prayer to a God who is personal becomes, not so much a talking to a person, as the expression of a quality of life in which the personal is being lived out in human relationships—an involvement of prayer rather than a speaking of prayer, but more of this later.

It may seem to the reader that I have taken a long bypath myself away from the subject of a relevant spirituality, but it has been a very necessary bypath. Because inevitably our view of prayer is bound up with our view of God, and the problem of what we mean by God, and above all what we mean by calling God personal, will obviously affect not only our beliefs about prayer but also the way in which we pray. Prayer and faith are inseparable both in content and in method.

CHAPTER 4

THE BACKGROUND OF MODERN PRAYER: THE LIMITATIONS OF THE CONCEPT OF PRAYER

So we come to the third section of the difficulties we encounter in thinking of prayer today. We are confused both in what we mean by God and also in what we mean by prayer. A report by a group of clergy and laity who met in a similar Conference at Sheffield to the one from which I have quoted at Maidstone to discuss the subject of "Spirituality in the Modern World" said:

> "What do you mean by prayer?" was shouted from one or other corner of the room whenever the word was mentioned. At least we learnt not to expect easy answers, nor even easy honesty on our own part in a topic that touches each of us in a very personal and deep way. This is because we recognize, perhaps, that we are talking about what really is "fundamental to the maintenance of truly human living" as well as because of guilt-feelings about broken rules.

We have so closely defined what we mean by prayer as talking to God that in this talking we have, as it were, certain rules of the conversation: it must contain elements of Praise, Confession, Thanksgiving, Intercession and Petition: we must give a certain time when relieved from the pressures of daily life, for this kind of talking; and the main distinction between the monastic, the secular cleric and the layman lies in the amount of time which is put aside—the monastic is expected to give most time because his life is orientated round this exercise, the parish priest is also expected to give set times each day because he too has the leisure for this, and the layman is expected to give least time. But it is all conceived in basically the same way: the norm of most of the manuals and most of the directions which come from spiritual directors is to take the monastic pattern and "water" it down successively for secular clergy and for laity. (Many a young priest today is beginning to revolt against this kind of "monastic imposition" in the devotional routine of his theological colleges.) Neither the manuals of dogmatic, mystical and ascetic theology of the Catholic nor the pietistic individualism of Protestant extempore or books of prayers speak to the needs of many today. I personally once tried hard to use the Ignatian and Sulpician methods of meditation and found, rather as the Preface to the Prayer Books says, that it was harder to remember how to meditate than to meditate when the method was found!

But there is a deeper sense than all this in which we have narrowed the concept of prayer, namely, the idea of prayer as disengagement from the world and therefore a sort of retreat time done in set places and at set times when the ordinary engagements of the day are over. This and its results have been well put by George MacLeod in *Only One Way Left* when he says:

> What debilitates our prayer life, I suggest, is our presupposition that the pressures of life are on one side while God is on some other side: interested and concerned but on some other side. With this supposition when evening comes with an ending to those pressures we are apt to go eagerly to God—disconcertingly to find a vacuum. We seek to fill the vacuum with "spiritual thoughts". The more we try, the more desperate does the situation become, till in effect we say we are not really the praying type. There are, of course, evenings when our prayer life is refreshing: but, analysed, they turn out to be the times when the pressures have been so weighty that you have simply had to go with them to God. The religious moment flows from the practical. Of the prayer life, too, we can come to say, "Hereby know we that we have passed from death to life because we love the brethren."

Is, then, one of the difficulties about prayer which makes it dead for many people that what we call prayer-life is separated from ordinary life, that it has become a matter of filling in the gaps with God rather than regarding the day's involvements as done in the presence of God. In which case, a far better definition of prayer than talking to God would be seeking to do the will of God, which would mean that training in prayer would be not training in how to talk to God but training in how to *know* His will for each day, and how to *respond* to that knowledge in the daily involvements: praying would then be a matter of *in* God rather than *to* God, letting Him *in* us review and appraise what we are and where we are, and then carrying that union with Him consciously into the relationships and activities which will constitute the day. This is to make real in daily living the advice of St Augustine, "Ask nothing of God, save God himself." We have imagined that unless we are saying set prayers we are not praying, but have we not unduly stylized and made religious what is really a matter for living, a living within the perspective of a life lived consciously in God? Father Besnard, a Roman Catholic Dominican, in an article on *Tendencies of Contemporary Spirituality* (*Concilium*, Vol. 9, No. 1) says:

> We conceive of spirituality as the search for a refined religiosity that is lived for its own sake, the doctrines of which may be correct in theory, but which betray their emptiness by diverting us from an integral Christian life . . . on the other hand spirituality may mean something *lived* in a most personal, serious way—the integral life that faith in Jesus Christ gives us as we live in *this* century, among *these* men, in *this* world. The spirituality sought by the Christian today is above all a spirituality to be lived . . . the language with which God speaks to man and man to God is not primarily words, but rather daily events, those choices that souls are continually called to make because of their very existence and which the Incarnation has shown us as not only the life of man, but the life of Christ in man, and yet no less the life of Christ.

In these words, it seems to me, are summed up the attitude underlying the search for a new meaning to prayer, a new way of praying, and a spirituality relevant to the needs of modern man. The human being of the twentieth century may not be so different basically from the human being of the first or seventeenth century but the environment and thinking of today is vastly different from that of former centuries. In the twentieth century men still seek for God, but the likelihood is that they will need twentieth century ways of finding him.

I have taken up much time with the background which gives rise to our difficulties about prayer today: the background which is part sociological, the characteristics of present-day society, part theological, the changing concepts of God, and part definitive, the meaning of the word "prayer". This. however, is vital to our task. The prophet Ezekiel, when asked to go and preach to the Jews in captivity, said first: "I sat where they sat." This is always a salutary thing to do: to start from the full understanding of the situation in which we find ourselves and with awareness of the reality of our difficulties is itself the necessary beginning to the much more difficult task of the search for a relevant spirituality today. Now, however, that search must begin, and I will start at the fountain-head of our faith and examine the prayer-life of Christ and his own teaching on prayer as the guide for authentic spirituality "in this century, and in this world".

CHAPTER 5

CHRIST AT PRAYER AND PRAYING IN CHRIST

It is customary to end formal liturgical prayer with the words, "through Jesus Christ our Lord": this is because, if the true nature of prayer is that prayer is in God rather than to God, then, since our knowledge of what the Being of God is comes to us through Jesus Christ, prayer is seeking to be in Christ and to be filled with the fullness of Him who filleth all in all as St Paul teaches us. To experience prayer is to experience what praying in Christ means.

First, however, let us consider what place prayer had for Christ and what He understood by prayer as revealed in His own prayer life, for then we shall begin to see what the "in-Christ" prayer will mean for us.

If we look at the pattern of the prayer-life of Christ we shall find that it falls into two categories: these are what we might call His times of withdrawal and His times of involvement, although often the latter are not called prayer at all. The times of withdrawal fall into three kinds of occasions. First, the times when withdrawal was essential in order that some agonizing reality of life might be dealt with or some agonizing question of ministry and servanthood, or of tormented wrestling with the understanding of the will of God; such occasions were the time of the Temptations in the Wilderness, the time of the Transfiguration, and the time in Gethsemane. Secondly, there are what might be called the withdrawals for the normal purposes of recouping strength, of quietly recollecting the day or anticipating the strain and problems of the morrow. Many such occasions are recorded in the Gospels: "He went up the hillside to pray alone. It grew late and he was there by himself" (Matt. 14: 22, 23; Mark 6: 46); "Very early next morning he got up and went out. He went away to a lonely spot and remained there in prayer" (Mark 1: 35); "and from time to time he would withdraw to lonely places for prayer" (Luke 5: 16); "One day when he was praying alone in the presence of his disciples he asked them, Who do people say I am?" (Luke 9: 18) (clearly on that occasion the meaning of His ministry was very much in His thoughts during His time of quiet); "Once in a certain place Jesus was at prayer. When he ceased one of his disciples said, Lord, teach us to pray" (Luke 11: 1–4). This last is an interesting example since clearly there was something in our Lord's way of praying which differed from the normal traditional praying of a Jew or the disciples would not have asked such a question. Thirdly, there are the withdrawals for some special purpose clearly indicated by what follows the withdrawal, of which one of the best examples is the whole night He spent in prayer before choosing the disciples: "He went out one day into the hills to pray and spent the night in prayer to God. When day broke he called his disciples to him and from among them he chose twelve." Quite clearly such a decision required a very great deal of prior thinking and right judgement so that He might make the choice of those who, despite their human failings, had it within them to be mature and true people and able to convey the truth of the meaning of life to others after Christ's own earthly departure.

There is a sense in which we can say that all the times of withdrawal prayer which are recorded of Christ are times of wrestling with the knowledge of what the will of God meant for Him, what the cost of the redemption of the world would mean, what being true man meant. Dietrich Bonhoeffer says:

> To be a Christian is to be a man. To be a Christian does not mean to be religious in a particular way, to cultivate some particular form of asceticism, but to be a man. It is not some religious act which makes a Christian what he is but participation in the suffering of God in the life of the world. (*Letters and Papers from Prison*, p. 166)

It is that experience of unity with God which was constantly both the joy and the suffering of Christ: it led Him to be driven by the Spirit into the wilderness because the moment that a man is going to be seriously used by God he will be driven out into the wilderness, he will be driven into the wilderness of the discovery of his real self (i.e. the reality of God in him), tormented by the demons of the false self which will constantly try to hide the real in the superficial: this tormenting and yet important act of self-discovery can only be done in solitude:

> Solitude affords the occasion for the supreme battle, and the only one that can be truly decisive. All the pretences, all the false trappings of demi-virtues in which he placed his trust, now fall away in a flash. He must see himself, recognize himself for what he is. He must transfer the struggle from the superficial levels of his being, from the mirages of the world or the phantoms of the flesh, to the darkened abysses of his own will which is only a will enslaved. Then each man finds revealed to him that the strength of God is fulfilled in our weakness, that His grace is sufficient for us, that it is when we are weakest that we are strong . . . it is only when a man has gone through this trial that he can say with his lips: "It is no longer I who live but Christ who lives in me." (Bouyer, *Introduction to Spirituality*, p. 205)

This is constantly the temptation of Christ, as it will be of the Christ in us: He must examine the reality of the ministry which is to be offered, that it consist not in the false trappings of superficial popularity, provision of easy reform, parade of power, even parade of religion—the easy gimmicks which lead straight from the truth of what is real to the superficial glitter of what is worldly success.

Then we find that Christ is engaged in the agony of the cost of redemption: we are not always aware in these days, when we so easily talk of love, of what the in-Christ love will mean in terms of cost. Of this Our Lord was always aware, as in us today He is always aware: that great stress and suffering can only be faced if a man has faced up to his true self, has discovered whether he has it in him to have the courage to be true even when everything is loaded against him, has in silence examined his own weaknesses, acknowledged them and so found victory over them. "If it be thy will, let this cup pass from me"—this must be understood, the shrinking must be faced and accepted, there must be no pretence, no hiding behind what I think I am. Otherwise in the time of testing there will be collapse and failure. Moreover, the cost of redemption includes the cost of letting oneself be the butt of hatred that men may find their release on the Christ in us. Participation in Christ means that willed love which has accepted that only by self-acceptance and self-emptying can one hope to be able to say with any truth: "Nevertheless, not my will but thine be done."

This, then, is one side of the prayer life of Christ and, therefore, of necessity will be one side of the in-Christ prayer life of ourselves, for this means that kind of wrestling with life which is only possible in the solitude when we in Him do as He did in His own incarnation—when we are trying to find out what God is doing in history, what is the meaning of what we are and what we are doing, what is the cost involved in the saying of "amen" to all this and what is the grace by which we are able to say "amen".

The other half of the prayer life of Christ is also the other half of our own prayer life—the half which is the carrying through of all this in the involvements of daily life, the half which is, in the words of Bonhoeffer, "being a man, participation in the suffering of God in the life of the world", or, to refer back to the words of Father Besnard, "the integral life that faith in Christ Jesus gives us as we live in *this* century, among *these* men, in *this* world". For Christ in His incarnation every activity in life was prayer, for every activity in life is an expression of the work of reconciling men to the reality which is their own true nature, reconciling men to the Being from which they had become estranged. When He is healing, He expresses His prayer in the work of healing, of bringing to the disease which is an expression of the unreal, of that which is false and un-natural, the restoration of the real, the wholeness, the life which is the true nature of the flesh. When He is teaching, He is involved in prayer, for He is involved in bringing to men the knowledge of their own meaning and purpose in life: the way, the truth and the life, which is theirs for the having, if they will only come to accept it. When He is forgiving, He is showing men what it means to be estranged from the ground of their being, He is restoring them to their true selves, the self which is accepted and therefore can learn to give that acceptance to others—it is not so much a form of words as an expression of the action of the eternal on the temporal. When He is comforting people in the ordinary circumstances of life, in conversation and in social meeting, He is praying because He is making them conscious of their true selves, helping them to strip from themselves the masks and facades which conceal their true selves, helping them to face and accept the truth about themselves, so that they may go further and become what they are meant to be: "perfect as their father in heaven is perfect".

In everything Christ does He is praying, because He is *meeting people with the truth*, He is bringing ultimate reality into the daily reality. He is by His very presence revealing the whole meaning of life, and this is prayer—the searching out of God in the human situation, which means the searching out of what truly *is*, of what truly is eternal in the human situation. The truth Christ proclaimed was Himself in the midst of life conveyed by healing, teaching, forgiving, understanding, identification with life in its joys and its sorrows. His only formalizing of all that in words of prayer is often by gesture or by one sentence holding up all that He is and is doing to God: the gestures of "looking upwards", "blessing", "offering thanks", "laying on of hands", or the summing up of all that is being done in the single words and sentences from the Cross.

The Prayer Life in Christ as Taught in the Lord's Prayer

The pattern of the Christ-prayer is also the pattern which He Himself taught us in the Lord's Prayer. When the disciples, struck by the difference between His manner of praying and the traditional Jewish praying to which they were accustomed, asked their question He gave them what has ever since been called the Lord's Prayer. But what is the Lord's Prayer? It is simply perspective first, then the result of perspective ,involvement; we are called to do three things: to hallow the name of God, to advance the reign of God, and to fulfil the will of God where we are. The Lord's Prayer is not really a prayer in the sense of a form of words: its very brevity speaks against the idea that prayer is mainly a matter of words. Rather is it like saying to those who asked Him: this is what life is like, this is how the reality of life is found.

First you set all in the perspective of the eternal: only in the beginning with Him and His hallowing can a proper appraisal of daily experience be healthily made. "Our Father, who art in heaven, hallowed be thy name": here is the nature of what is expressed as personal, transcendent, and immanent—that is, both revealed in the personal expressed by the nature of a father, and in the beyond in the midst of the "who art in heaven" (the natural language of that age to express the eternal breaking into the temporal): you learn to hallow His name, which is to hallow the being which is His creation and of which He is the ground. You learn to hallow the "I am that I am", to hallow all that is, so that in that hallowing we have the right perspective from the start of our daily involvements, namely that the whole of God's creation is sacred; there is no division of the sacred and the secular. To quote the words of Teilhard de Chardin:

> By virtue of the creation and still more of the Incarnation nothing here below is profane for those who know how to see. On the contrary everything is sacred to the men who can distinguish that portion of chosen being which is subject to Christ's drawing power in the process of consummation. Try with God's help to perceive the connection which binds your labour with the building of the kingdom of heaven. May the time come when men having awakened to a sense of the close bond linking all the movements of the world in the single, all-embracing work of the Incarnation shall be unable to give themselves to any one of their tasks without illuminating it with the clear vision that their work is received and put to good use by a Centre of the universe . . . to experience the attraction of God, to be sensible of the beauty, the consistency and the final unity of being is the highest and at the same time the most complete of our passivities of growth. (*Le Milieu Divin*, p. 40)

Teilhard de Chardin puts in more beautiful language than I could ever express the perspective by which all our earthly involvements are hallowed. Michel Quoist puts it perhaps more simply, expressing the meaning of "Hallowed be thy name" as follows:

> I would understand that nothing is secular, neither things nor people nor events
> But that on the contrary everything has been made sacred in its origin by God
> And that everything must be consecrated by man made divine.

So the first thing that Our Lord puts before us is that *life must start with the right perspective*: all things are an expression of the divine reality, the hallowed name which is the name "I am that I am", the name of all Being, and this hallowing is found in the Now of life, the presence of God in His world. So if we are to find what is the meaning of the now of our own day we must first look at that now in the light of the Eternal Now. The eternal dimension is the necessary beginning to understanding and living the true life. The hallowing of creation means that not only do we see all things as the revelation of the work of God, even the humblest things of life, but that you cannot start out on the day unless you start by making yourself sensible to and understanding of the inner meaning of life, the sacredness of all life because God's name is hallowed and God is Being and, therefore all being is hallowed. A remarkable illustration of this hallowing of God in the ordinary details of life is given by George MacLeod in a conversation from a Zen Buddhist monastery. A business man at the monastery is conversing with a monk:

> *Business Man:* Ever since I came I have had no instruction in the meaning of reality.
> *Monk:* Ever since you came I have been instructing you.
> *Business Man:* In what way?
> *Monk:* When you brought tea, did I not accept it? When you served me food did I not eat it? When you made bows to me did I not return them? When did I ever neglect to give you instruction?
> *Business Man:* What is reality?
> *Monk:* Walk on.
> *Business Man:* What is realization?
> *Monk:* Your every-day thoughts.
> *Business Man:* What is the one ultimate word of truth?
> *Monk:* Yes. (*Only One Way Left*, p. 158)

If this conversation is as perplexing to you as it seems to have been to the business man, then realize that what the monk is saying is that the reality of God is *now* as life is *now*: it is not in some rarified religious sphere but in the most simple details of ordinary life that the reality which is God is seen. Our task is to say "Yes" as the one ultimate word of truth to that nowness of God, to say, like the Beatles, "Yea, Yea, Yea" to God in every moment of daily life, in every decision we make, in every conversation, in every act of forgiveness or acceptance, in every desire for guidance, in every determination to meet the needs of people. It is the ultimate word of truth because it is the word of commitment, of commitment to the Reality of God in the daily realities of life.

If we see the hallowing of God's name as the revelation of the work of God in all creation, the making of the secular the sacred, then it follows in the way of spirituality revealed through the Lord's Prayer that the next step will be the affirmation of what that means in terms of our servanthood in the world. So on to "Thy kingdom come, thy will be done". Thy kingdom come is the expression of the ultimate evolution of the universe and all that is in it to the point at which in all life there is expressed that which is already given in the life of Jesus Christ, namely the obedience of all things to God. If there is no division between the sacred and the secular, there is equally nothing which is not to be brought under the rule of God, whether we call it religious or secular: the life of Christ expresses the meaning of the Kingdom, for in Christ and His obedience is the representation of what the Kingdom means, and in the symbolism of the Ascension is the interpretation for the disciples of what the task for them now is as the embodiment of the Body of Christ. As in Christ the meaning of the kingdom is seen, so in His Church the meaning of the kingdom is to be worked out within the secular city. This is our task and this is the direct following upon the hallowing of God.

How is this task to be done? Through the operation of wills that have become one with the will of God, and our prayer life will be the life which affirms and confirms that unity whose effectiveness will be in proportion to the sincerity of its utterance. To pray "Thy will be done" is to *desire* the accomplishment of God's will in *all* life. Therefore, personal prayer should not be telling God what we think He should know because He is "out there", but rather seeking to know what is His will and to be enabled with the help of grace to do it. If Christ is the embodiment of the Kingdom, and if the work of the Kingdom is now the responsibility of His Body the Church, then to pray is to seek to be in Christ and to be filled with all the fullness of God. But this is not just an individual matter, because the will of God is not a matter of various individuals giving conflicting answers and saying, "But this is the will of God *for* me." This would be to make the will of God purely a subjective interpretation of individual believers, and we have had some very strange claims in the past by individuals who claimed that they had a kind of private access to the will of God! Our individual vocation in this respect is subordinate to the vocation of the whole body. If we pray to know God's will, this implies that God's will is already known: it is in the person of Christ, in the understanding of the universality of love. But what love means in terms of any particular situation or human context is something which of necessity must be worked out through the Church acting through small groups meeting together to thresh out and think out what is the will of God within their existing situation.

When a group meets together to work out what being a Christian means in a particular situation, this means that the will of God is being sought within the limits of the knowledge of God already revealed through the Scriptures. The seeking of the will of God is not then a matter of God "speaking" back to a person saying his or her prayers, but the attempt of the Body represented through its members to discover what is already there—namely the will of God—and to conform their wills to it. So this often means that we have to lay aside previous values and loyalties because in the Kingdom, that is, in the new life of Christ, there is the new reality of life lived according to God's will for the bringing in of His kingdom. So the seeking to know the will of God is not a kind of private conversation with God in which He reveals His will to me, but rather the corporate group which is the Body of Christ seeking to know what being in-Christ means in terms of the particular secular experience with which they are dealing.

But this will also be a purgative experience for the group: for, if our wills in the daily experiences and communications of life are to be conformed to the will of God, this will mean that prayer and ascesis go hand in hand: in order to be filled with God we must first be empted of ourselves and this is a painful experience: "he has no beauty that we should desire him". Following the will of God has very little to do with sweet feelings and pleasant glows of personal communion with God: it is much more likely to produce the real disturbance of casting off of preconceived prejudices, class-motivated thinking, cherished facades, which will be the ascesis of a group trying to express in modern society the will of God.

The first part of the Lord's Prayer, then, gives both the perspective in which life is to be lived—the hallowing of all that is, the name of God—and the mission which is the whole life of obedience to the will of God where God has placed us in the world. What are the essentials of that mission in terms of everyday existence? The rest of the Lord's Prayer provides the answer. They may be summed up in three ways: daily service, daily acceptance, daily guidance. The spirituality which results from a proper perspective on life and a proper following of the will of God is a spirituality of involvement in the issues of the day, a spirituality in which the whole man is being the servicing, reconciling and guiding Christ to the life of His world, "doing everything in word or deed in the name of the Lord Jesus" (Colossians 3:17).

Daily Service

The terms in which Our Lord expresses the daily involvement of service are very simple: "Give us this day our daily bread." Nothing could be more practical. Prayers in the Bible are very rarely prayers for the general welfare of people: they are for particular needs. It costs little to pray for all men according to their needs; it costs much more to pray for the needs we know in the brother we know, for we shall immediately see that to pray for daily bread means to be concerned with daily bread, to work for the satisfactions which are right and normal for all men. Bonhoeffer rightly protests against the kind of Christianity which looks upon God as a *deus ex machina* only able to help when men are weak and helpless and suffering and he says:

> I should like to speak of God not on the borders of life but at its centre, not in weakness but in strength, not, therefore, in man's suffering and death but in his life and prosperity . . . God is the beyond in the midst of life. (*Letters and Papers from Prison*, p. 12)

This is exactly what "Give us this day our daily bread" is doing—speaking to man in the midst of life, for what is more symbolic of the strength, the life, the prosperity, the joy of man than the daily needs of his life? The God who is in the midst of life concentrates our attention upon the right satisfactions of men in life—his food, his drink, his sexuality, his happiness, his strength and health; we are called to minister to those needs, whether they be a hunger for material food as in the East, or a hunger for meaning and mitigation of loneliness as all too often in the West. One is reminded of the words of St James: "If a brother or a sister be naked and destitute of daily food. And one of you say to them: Depart in peace, be ye warmed and filled: nothwithstanding ye give them not these things which are needful to the body: what doth it profit"? (James 2: 14–17), or again the words of Isaiah: "Is it such a fast that I have chosen? a day for a man to afflict his soul . . . is not this the fast that I have chosen? to loosen the bands of wickedness, to undo the heavy burdens . . . is it not to deal thy bread to the hungry and that thou bring the poor that are cast out to thy house." (Isa. 58: 6)

Prayer, then, is involvement of service which will carry us into the fields of politics, economics, welfare, social work; the spirituality which is in Christ will be a matter of practice rather than profession, as the Parable of the Sheep and the Goats indicates.

> The test is not the religious practice of the comfortable classes but the feeding of the hungry, the housing of the homeless, the visiting and acceptance of the prisoners and not their rejection. (Stanley Evans, *The Social Hope of the Christian Church*, p. 51)

Daily Acceptance

The next daily involvement to which Christ calls us, without which all human relationships of the day will fail, is "Forgive us our trespasses as we forgive them that trespass against us", the need for the understanding that we are accepted by God and the acceptance of others as they are. One of the most dangerous tendencies of Christian thinking has been to talk about *sins* rather than about sin, with the net result that we make ladders of sins—serious sins and not so serious sins; then stand ourselves reasonably comfortably half-way up the ladder, and although we may at times rather wistfully look up to the saints on the top rungs we more often look down comfortably to the (by conventional standards) disreputable sinners at the bottom, which gives us a nice feeling of some kind of merit if we have avoided the grosser sins! We so easily want to earn our forgiveness and it is a source of great distress to realize that we, in common with all sinners, are forgiven without any deservings. Or, alternatively, we hate what lies buried within us and try to pretend that it is not there and so present a facade to the world which is not really us but the self we approve of: it is often self-hate rather than self-love which tends both to destroy us and destroy those with whom we have relationships. We are estranged from ourselves and from others because we are estranged from God and have not accepted our forgiveness. We build up ladders of sins and find it difficult to accept those we think below us on the ladder, because we do not realize that in the sight of God we are all publicans and sinners with no distinctions between us. It is sin, not sins, for which we need and are given forgiveness. So the second petition of the Lord's Prayer sends us out into the world rejoicing in our acceptance by God and able, therefore, to accept others also. We make no claims for ourselves, we simply throw ourselves upon Christ: we make no pretences, we hide behind no useful facades, we are simply us in all our rags, the Rogues Gallery of humanity, not the Royal Academy of Saints, and yet just in that moment when we know our acceptance we are also the Royal Academy of Saints. Christ again in us has been with the publicans and sinners.

> It is as though a voice were saying: "You are accepted. You are accepted, accepted by that which is greater than you, and the name of which you do not know. Do not ask for the name now . . . simply accept the fact that you are accepted." (Tillich, *The Shaking of the Foundations*, p. 163)

So in the consciousness of that acceptance I can go into the world of daily relationships learning to love myself and to give myself true significance as a man, so that in the light of that I need not demand that others must become a certain type before I can accept them. I need not feel impelled to dominate or to possess, to make judgements, but rather learn that true relationship consists in giving to others the significance as human beings that we claim for ourselves: in other words the second clause of the Lord's Prayer is the carrying forth into human relationships of the command, "Love thy neighbour *as* thyself".

Daily Guidance

So we pass to the only other basic need of human living, the need for daily guidance. If I am to learn what servicing I am to do, what relationships I am to make during the day, I shall need to have that kind of realism about myself and the world in which I am that will help me to express "lead us not into temptation" and "deliver us from evil". This means that increasing self-knowledge which will enable us to know what kind of persons we really are, not what we think we are: we shall not hide behind some false self and persuade ourselves it is the truth or we shall be led into temptation because we do not know ourselves sufficiently well to know where for us lies temptation. It also means that we shall need to know the pressures with which we are surrounded so that from our knowledge of ourselves and of the pressures we shall know where the pressures are likely to be too much for us. So we shall seek to know what are the likely factors which affect our judgement of things—the class distinctions to which we are subject, the prejudices which mar our judgement, the dangers of status symbols, of other people's influence upon us, the kinds of company and circumstances which will be too much for us. We shall not necessarily avoid the pressures because we cannot, but we shall know that we have to deal with them and work through them in ourselves before we can carelessly throw ourselves in the way of them.

If the knowledge of ourselves and of the pressures of life awaken us to the dangers of temptation, so the realization that the source of all temptation is "ye shall be as gods" will cause us to go into the world with the desire "deliver us from evil". For the root evil is to take that short cut to divinity (which is in fact the ultimate goal of man who recognizes his dependence upon God) through arrogant trust in our own competence and capacity. Realizing, as I said earlier, that what is good is what conforms to the creative purposes of God working for the ultimate unity of all things, and that therefore what is evil is all that works away from unity and towards destruction whether of myself, others or society as a whole, I shall go out into the daily involvements of life with the conscious purpose of working for what is unitive and creative in work, in neighbourhood, in political life, in personal life. I shall know that to do this will involve my dependence upon the source of all unity, that it is not the trust in our own competence, in the pride of our own knowledge and strength that brings creative unity into life, but the recognition that in Christ is this unity to be sought: "He has made known to us his hidden purpose . . . namely that the universe, all in heaven and on earth might be brought into a unity in Christ . . . he put everything in subjection beneath his feet" (Ephesians 1: 9, 10, 22).

So it is fitting that the perspective with which the Lord's Prayer began should also be its end if the life of spirituality in the world is to be lived aright. If I am to be the servant of men's needs, the accepter of men as one accepted myself, the one aware of the guidance of self-knowledge and of the pressures of life, aware of my need for close dependence of communion if the evil of self and other destructiveness is to be avoided, I shall have towards the world the reverent adoration of the world set under God for the fulfilment of his purposes—"Thine is the kingdom, the power and the glory":

> Man having come into the full possession of his sphere of action, his strength, his maturity and his unity, will at last have become an adult

> being: and having reached this apogee of his responsibility and freedom, holding in his hands all his future and his past, will make the choice between arrogant autonomy and loving excentration. This will be the final choice: revolt or adoration of a world. (Teilhard de Chardin, *The Future of Man*, p. 19)

Perhaps this is the crucial distinction between the Christian and the humanist—the humanist cannot say: "*Thine* is the kingdom, the power and the glory" but rather "*Mine* is the kingdom, the power and the glory".

Finally, the whole perspective of the Lord's Prayer is in the setting of community: it is "*Our* Father, forgive *us*, lead *us*, deliver *us*." It is a group spirituality even more than an individual spirituality: it is not a pietistic individualism between my soul and God. It is rather an experience of living which I primarily find in and through others.

CHAPTER 6

THE FORM AND PRACTICE OF MODERN SPIRITUALITY

We may now begin to see to what all our previous thinking has been pointing in regard to forms of spirituality appropriate to the present day. All the paths we have been following lead to the same conclusions about the basic forms of a modern spirituality. The nature of the world in which we live presents us with a man in search of meaning to life, concerned existentially with his actions, his decisions, his involvement in human affairs, how he may understand himself. There is an emphasis upon the empirical in this life, what can be seen to work. There is a concentration upon the immanent and an impatience with the traditional. Yet there is a sense also of isolation, of loneliness, of being pressurized by crowds, of needing time to think and to adjust and to know how to cope with life. The mobility of life and the increasing anonymity of life leads him to want to understand what kind of relationships he should be making with people in various activities of life; he is increasingly involved in various groupings, and in wanting to make the groups work he is showing increasing interest in threshing out things with small groups. He is rejecting old forms of authority and discipline and yet realizing that the becoming of a whole or mature man is a costly business and it is necessary to learn what are the new forms of commitment which will enable him to find true freedom from pressures. He is beginning to realize that a society without any disciplines is unable to provide the right environment for freedom, for the resultant anarchy will simply produce a jungle in which the more sensitive go to the wall.

The debate about the meaning of God speaks also of the importance of meaning to life and thinks in terms of God as the ultimate meaning and reality behind life itself, as the ground of the existential being of man: it speaks of the refinding of the Hebraic rather than the Greek concept of the God who is found in the involvements of human living.

> There is a breaking down of the distinction between the sacred and the secular, the holy and the profane. The whole world is God's; it is his created order; the entire earth is the arena for his actions. Let us not, therefore, so runs the modern thinking, try to place him in special sacred places like Churches or tabernacles. He is in the world and we must find and serve him there. (John Coburn, *Contemporary Non-Catholic Spirituality*, article in *Worship*, Vol. 39, No. 10)

It speaks of the God whose nature is essentially personal and who is therefore to be discovered through the personal in human living: it speaks of the God whose gift of religious community in this age is the small group, whose Church seeks more and more to work through small groups: it speaks of the God who is constantly through history showing forth the costliness of love.

In the person of Christ we also see the same pattern: the Christ who in Himself incarnates the meaning of life and nature of authentic living, the Christ who relates that meaning of love and maturity of living to every sphere of human involvement, the Christ who accepts in Himself the costliness of that love, and who works thorough the small group in their own training in the holy worldliness which is living in the spirit in the world. The prayer life of Christ in which we share is the wrestling with the meaning and costliness of living in His withdrawals for this purpose, and the involvement with men when prayer is being acted out in living. The pattern of prayer again speaks first of meaning and perspective to life, then translates that into terms of personal self-understanding, and servicing of the world and the recognition that all this is done within human groupings—the "us" rather than the "I".

From all our thinking, then, there seem to emerge four basic necessities of a relevant spirituality:

(a) There must be the opportunity for thinking out and reflecting upon the meaning and the reality which lie behind our earthly living in the world. Irenaeus said: "The glory of God is man fully alive". If there is to be this kind of understanding of life, there must be the opportunity of standing back for a while from life, when in the silence of reflective thinking we may find in the dimension of eternity the meaning and the truth of our lives, in which we may learn to understand reality and to bear truth. Perhaps what we are striving for in modern contemplative prayer is expressed as well as it can be by one who would not normally be thought of as a religious writer, namely D. H. Lawrence:

> Thought, I love thought,
> But not the juggling and twisting of already existent ideas.
> I despise that self-important game.
> Thought is the welling up of unknown life into consciousness,
> Thought is the testing of statements on the touchstone of conscience,
> Thought is gazing on the face of life and reading what can be read,
> Thought is pondering over experience and coming to conclusion,
> Thought is not an exercise or a trick or a set of dodges,
> Thought is a man in his wholeness, wholly attending. (From *Last Poems*)

I know of no phrase which expresses more completely and succinctly the wrestling in reflective thinking with both what my wholeness in life is to be and my union with the eternal realities than "Thought is a man in his wholeness wholly attending".

(b) If our first action of prayer is the reflection upon the meaning of what I am doing, then the second is surely to carry that spirituality of reflection right into the doings of the world. Our vocation, and therefore our spirituality, is to be Christ to the world. We seek Christ where He is to be found in the stuff of daily life

How often do we sing:

> The daily round, the common task,
> Will furnish all we need to ask,
> Room to deny ourselves, a road
> To bring us daily nearer God.

and how often do we really listen to what we are singing, instead of haring off after methods of prayer! We get ourselves involved in religious practices, Lent Study courses, little manuals of prayers, and this is all a flight from the place where God speaks to us most plainly—in our daily bread. This is effective prayer—love in action—and certainly the layman's spirituality is the conscious seeing of Christ under the species of our daily bread and meeting Him where He encounters us in the world—in the pleasures as well as in the sorrows, in the health, strength and vigour of life as well as in the sufferings of life. This is where St Theresa of Lisieux has so much to teach us—her sanctification lay in the daily tasks, not in some other-worldly mysticism. So much of what we think of as prayer has turned it into something abstract and unrooted in the human condition and contemporary situation. It is by the way in which we respond to our human situation that we pray, for it is by the way of our response that we show the Christ in us to the world. Spirituality today does not mean having an occasional glance at God, or, after the activities of life are over, *saying* prayers. The language with which God speaks to man and man to God is not the language of formal words but rather the language of daily events, those choices that we are continually called to make because of our very existence, and which the Incarnation has shown us as not only the life of man but the life of Christ in man. It is in these encounters with others that we are, in the words of the Bishop of Woolwich, "praying for people, agonizing with God for them, precisely as we meet them and give our souls to them" (*Honest to God*, p. 99). Our prayer, then, of involvement with the world will be not a conversation with God but a conversation with the world, in which like the Jewish Psalmist and Prophet the divine intervention is being discovered. There will be no gap between the holy and the human, between the time of prayer and the time of engagement with the world, between commitment to the eternal and commitment to the temporal, between union with God and union with the world. Prayer will be the "cutting edge" of Christ worked out in the sphere of daily work ("the daily bread"), daily relationships ("forgive as forgiven"), daily resistance to destructive pressures ("lead us not into temptation, deliver us from evil"). If you say to me, "But this is not prayer, this is Christian living", I shall reply, "There is no differencc." What makes it prayer is that it is Christian living *consciously thought out* and *consciously motivated for Christ's sake*—"the thought of a man in his wholeness, wholly attending"—and then wholly acting for God in his world and in man's. Teilhard de Chardin writes:

> The general run of the faithful feel that the time spent at the office, in the studio, in the fields or in the factory is time taken away from prayer and adoration. Under the sway of these feelings large numbers of Catholics have led a double or crippled life in practice: they have to step out of their human dress so as to have faith in themselves as Christians and inferior Christians at that . . . Christianity is not, as it is sometimes presented and sometimes practised, an additional burden of observances and obligations but an immense power which bestows significance, beauty and a new lightness upon *what we are already doing*.
>
> (*Le Milieu Divin*, pp. 37, 43)

(c) *But we must also remember that living this life of prayer-involvement in the world brings its own recognition of the costliness of Christian living.* In a world where the ethos of life is not so much daily bread for all as daily cake for all, where the emphasis is upon indulgence and ease and affluence, there is the great danger that this kind of ethos will also invade our spirituality; we may fling away our office books and our set patterns of prayers as simply a glorious excuse to be free of all that is not simply comfortable and pleasant. If the only difference that the world sees between the Christian and the non-Christian is that one goes to church and one does not, but that in life both are serving Mammon, the Christian as conditioned to ease of worldliness as everyone else, then the Cross of Christ will have disappeared from spirituality and so will any relevance of Christian living. It is only when we are bearing Christ's cross, dying daily, that we are living fully as Christians and suffering with the world's sufferings—*com*passion and *com*munion. There is a proper place for asceticism, for the modern equivalent of fasting, and this also must be part of a relevant spirituality. If, then, we are seeking to ask the question in the modern world, "What is a Christian?" we shall be compelled to consider as part of a revelant spirituality what is the relevant modern style of poverty, chastity, obedience, mortification and fasting. Asceticism is almost a loaded word, but in all our talk about love we may not always suspect the price that must be paid if we are to love in-Christ.

(d) The last characteristic we must note in a contemporary spirituality is the tendency of modern life in its search for meaning and wholeness to turn away from individualism and solitary paths to a search for the group whose objectives correspond to aspirations and needs. In the search for mental wholeness the psychologist has discovered the value of group therapy, the sociologist seeks to discover what is a meaningful social grouping in an area, and in the Church there is increasing demand for lay training institutes, in which group study may be conducted, together with learning of group relationships. We sense in the mobility of modern society the need for understanding the different kinds of group relationships which must be made, and in an impersonal and increasingly anonymous society there is a deep consciousness of the need for community. This is a phenomenon constantly associated with spirituality—the monastic communities, the little brothers of St Francis, the reformed communities of Carmel in the sixteenth century, the Bruderhof experiments in Germany, the Kibbutz of Israel, the Taizé Community—all these are demonstrations of the need for a spirituality to be expressed in terms of community experience. We need the brother near at hand who will understand what we are trying to do, will support us in the doing of it, and will come to the help of the brother who needs that support. We are all too well aware of the lack of such support within the categories of our Church congregational life. We shall therefore want to discover how our spiritual life is to be expressed in community today: what are the ways by which such community can contribute both to the understanding of ourselves and the reality in which we are grounded and which in daily involvement we are working out. Father Besnard, in the article I have previously quoted, puts this whole search for community as follows:

> Christians seeking to carry out their evangelical aspirations, feel the crying need for a community where they will be able to realize

certain great values of the Gospel, such as were shown by the primitive community in Jerusalem. They want, as they say, to "incarnate" these values, to render them tangible; they are not to be satisfied with talking about them, but in living them. They instinctively understand that the community is the Gospel made visible. A shared life, modest perhaps but real: a fraternal communion which has an inner structure of human friendship that is quite palpable; a prayer which in order to be the prayer of several people does not cease to be the prayer of each: here are the many requirements that seek satisfaction in the new groups, necessarily and vitally linked to, but not identifiable with, the associations of their local Churches. (*Tendencies of Contemporary Spirituality* in *Concilium*, Vol. 9, No. 1)

These, then, are the four basic elements of a contemporary relevant spirituality—a time for reflection upon life, a consciousness of an in-Christ involvement in life, an asceticism appropriate to the witness of the costliness of love in the secular world, and the "religious community" which reflects man's proper solidarity of spirit serving the wider community. The next task will be to see how each one of these may be developed in practical terms: what each means for us in the realization of a pattern of spirituality that will bring the eternal into the presence of the now.

CHAPTER 7

THE NEEDS OF PRAYER AND LIVING

In thinking out the practice of a relevant spirituality I do not wish to overthrow one lot of rules and regulations concerning times and places of prayer for another. Nor do I wish, in abandoning the concept of prayer as talking to God, to substitute another definition to which the form of prayer must subscribe. Rather do I want to see the interaction of reflection and living as the way by which the very life of God within us is seeking to find its expression against all that stands in the way of that expression. At one of our training week-ends for the laity a cry came from the heart of one of those present: "I have been trying for years to work on the patterns of prayer laid down in the devotional books but what I really want to know is how to pray my life, not how to use fifteen minutes cut out of life." The basic elements of a relevant contemporary spirituality are concerned with this very request—"how to pray my life".

A Time for Reflection Upon Life (*Contemplation*)

I have put in brackets the word Contemplation in this time for reflection upon life because if prayer is the act of God working within us then this is traditionally the meaning of the term Contemplation—namely the direct action of God upon the soul. In traditional terminology, the direct action of God upon the soul is described as having three stages—the Purgative, that from which we need to be freed or released; the Illuminative, that which illuminates the faith in relation to our living so that our existence is enlightened by our understanding of the relationship of the truth of God to life; and the Unitive, in which the life of the Spirit can begin in the world in union with God's will for the world.

First then in this time for reflection, the breaking through of the reality which is God is the breaking through into my own consciousness of the reality which is myself. I shall need constantly to seek for the greatest degree of self-awareness, the maximum of honesty in the understanding of what in me is hindering the showing of the reality of God to others, what in me is unreal. The breaking through of God in my time of reflection is the *purgative* experience of discovering what is unreal, empty, superficial, the poses both pious and otherwise. A Dominican has put it thus: "What we are worth when motionless is the question."

We also seek to discover what are the self-imposed prisons we are making for ourselves: what are the prejudices, the preconceived ideas, the class conditionings which prevent us from seeing things as they really are; as Michel Quoist so truly puts it:

> Locked in myself
> Prisoner of myself
> I hear nothing but my voice
> I see nothing but myself (*Prayers of Life*, p. 87)

This purgative experience we must have so that we may learn to accept ourselves and see ourselves as we are and realize that this is the self which God accepts and forgives. Yet this is the self through which God works, and He will work but dimly if there is little reality in the understanding I have of myself. This will be my prayer of Confession, not in the enumeration of sins but rather in the honest presentation of the whole sinful man which is me to the ultimate reality which is my true self. In order to be able to have this kind of realistic understanding of ourselves, we shall need to expose ourselves to the seeing of others, to be able to accept the criticisms which we are given, to have the opportunities of speaking the truth in love to each other, and also to have as basic an understanding of the forces which motivate us both without and within as we can, both by experience and by understanding of modern psychology and sociology.

If the purgative experience in terms of seeking to pierce the unrealities of ourselves is a must for the time of reflection, then so is the *illuminative* experience, in which we are letting the illumination of reality cast its searchlight over the world and the activities into which we are going during that day or the next day. This is essentially what the *Prayers* of Michel Quoist are doing: they are not in the traditional sense of the word prayers at all, but they speak with great meaning to people, as I have discovered from using them in schools and universities, because they start with human situations and bring to bear upon them the reflections of Biblical insights, holding up those situations to the searchlight of the reality of God. They are reflections upon the meaning of life rooted in and starting from the situations.

George MacLeod puts this kind of reflective thinking and illuminative experience very well when he writes:

> In the morning we resolutely count out the paper money of our plotted day till we have assessed its value in the coinage of the eternal. In the light of the Incarnation nothing is secular. But unless we handle each paper token of the seeming secular and hold it till we see its true value in the light of the glorified humanity, then by ten of the morning we are down one precipice of the knife-edge and are in like judgement with the pietist who has gone down the other side. (*Only One Way Left*, p.161)

What he means by the two sides of the precipice is that it is as possible to fall from the true illumination on life by either excessive activity without proper reflection as it is by excessive piety separated from living. The Bishop of Woolwich speaks of the same kind of activity when he says, "We see the diary in depth, we prepare in the telephone to meet our God." (*Honest to God*, p. 101)

Perhaps for the clergy, in place of the formal recitation of the offices, there might be a daily Communion and then, by that illumination of reality which the presence of Christ in the Communion brings upon the daily bread and wine of life, they might spend time in reflection upon the diary, the difficult engagements of the day, the meetings and people which are going to be awkward, the difficult letter and the morning paper, while still in the church. To let the light of truth shine upon them, the presence of Christ come into them in advance of the involvement, to let the wholeness of wholly attending be given to them, this would be to make the pattern of our reflection the pattern of our engagement. This might well be followed by a group Bible study at the vicarage, in which the reflections gained in the time of silence upon the daily events of both world and neighbourhood might be pooled in the light of a Biblical study which seeks to understand the eternal meaning behind these events. For the layman it might mean letting the journey to town, or the reflections of the night before, be given to the same consideration of the diary and the engagement pad.

So we shall be preparing ourselves in the time of reflection for the *unitive* experience, the third stage in spiritual living, when we shall be able to be engaged with the world in a living union with the will of God for the world. We shall be beginning to understand how the situations of a secular life may be faced and answered in unity with and not in separation from God. What is the Christian action I must take? What will this mean for others? How can God's will be done by me through this day? These are the unitive questions of daily living.

When we study the Bible to seek the answers to these questions, it takes on a very different relevance from our normal Biblical reading. We are no longer ploughing steadily through in accordance with the requirements of a lectionary, but rather seeking to find within its pages the understanding of the truth about ourselves and the truth about our daily living. We are studying in order that we may daily experience something of the mystical unitive experience, working through the lack of meaning at the different levels of life until we come to a surer and more certain knowledge of the truth, the way and the life, which lies behind all existential living.

There is one other important way in which the time for reflection will often need to be used, which should probably have come within the realm of the purgative experience. Earlier I spoke of the Cross as the means by which Christ allowed men to release their hatreds upon Himself. I believe that the sweat of agony in the Garden of Gethsemane was part of the great and necessary preparation to be able to take upon Himself the sins of the world: He had to feel as His own the destructive forces which lie within us, the aggression, the self-hate, the malice, the despair, in order that there might be full redemption of the self that lies buried within us as well as the self we present at the surface. Is it not an extension of this agony that the moment Christ was most closely united with the source of His own being was the moment at which He cried, "My God, my God, why hast thou forsaken me?" Is not our true identification with Christ when we accept His acceptance of ourselves in all our own darkness, in all the nastiness of what we are, in our rages, our self-pity, our resentments, and when in the full awareness of our sense of separation from God we release those hatreds upon Him, we work off the evils of which we re conscious and we do not try to pretend that because we do not like them they must not be shown. Is not this feeling of utter deprivation of God, of resentment against God, of loss even of faith itself (or apparent loss), of the valuelessness of ourselves, of utter darkness, something akin to the dark night of the soul of which St John of the Cross speaks, and is not the deep psychological understanding (by modern standards of psychology) of what lies buried within us which St John shows, because both the Saint of the Middle Ages and the twentieth century psychologist who may call himself an agnostic are in fact expressing some of the deepest truths about the nature of man, and in Christ those deepest truths are eternally incarnated?

Let us then use our time for reflection sometimes, when necessary, as times for rage. There will be times when I want to rage against God and to express my deep dissatisfactions with myself and with my life. To try to pretend that these do not exist, or to suppress them because they are considered blasphemous, is to indulge in unreal pretence, to be less than myself. Modern plays often blaspheme against God, and we are shocked, and pious people demand censorship; we should recognize that such blasphemy is itself a necessary release and often a necessary protest and the rage is redemptive both for those who express it and for those who hear it. I know that there are times when, consumed with frustration or with resentment or with that self-pity which can be more destructive than anything else in life, I have simply gone into church and knelt before the Blessed Sacrament and poured out on Christ all that lay within me. I have not said what piety demanded I should say but what I really wanted to say. I have experienced to the full the love-hate relationship with God: the faith which impels me to pour out before the one that at that moment I hated the expression of that hatred and yet knowing somehow, even in the moment of hating, that it is before God alone that I am really free to do this. I have known that it is the Christ who cried out, "My God, my God, why hast thou forsaken me?" who in me now cries out the same, knowing that only when I have released this sense of utter separation from God shall I be able to find life again. The Christ who has said, "Come unto me all ye that travail and are heavy laden and I will refresh you" has done that very thing. Heavy laden with bitterness and resentment I have, when it is allowed to become known to me and consciously expressed, been able to find the release which is its own refreshing.

There are many examples of this kind of release which one could quote. To mention a few: Fénelon once wrote, "If God bores you, tell him so." St Teresa describes her exasperation with God when she cried, "I do not wonder, God, that you have so few friends from the way you treat them." Michel Quoist in *The Prayer of a Priest on Sunday Night* speaks of the feelings of frustration and loneliness which befall a celibate priest, and protests angrily against the amount of love he is expected to give others in, "Lord, why did you tell me to love?" The Don Camillo stories speak very humanly of the resentment which Don Camillo often has against God. One of the finest illustrations of this kind of release is to be found in a powerful novel by Peter de Vries, *The Blood of the Lamb*. The hero of the novel, Wanderhope, has gone into a church on his way to the hospital to see his daughter who is dying of leukaemia; he has gone to pray for her recovery; it is the child's birthday and he takes with him a birthday cake. When he arrives at the hospital he finds the child dying and soon afterwards dies. He returns to the church and throws the cake at the crucifix and in that action finds his release.

These, then, are the ways by which we may use the time for reflection: the ways of self-understanding, life-understanding, peace through release-understanding. They are ways by which alone we may safely go into the world and its involvements because we shall then go with the right perspective on life—as in the Lord's Prayer: "God and His hallowing": we shall have faced as many aspects of ourselves and of our experiences as we can, and made our choice for the creative rather than the destructive. If we do not take time to do this, we shall be caught in the tread-mill of our own experiences; we shall be caught and dragged along by everything that happens; we shall become that most terrible spectacle of all—the priest or layman who rushes hither and thither, is always "busy", but who never has time for himself or for others—the irrelevant and superficial activist who is the current menace in much of our Church life, dabbling in all things but knowing nothing. Oscar Wilde once put it thus:

> While in the opinion of the world contemplation is the gravest sin of which any citizen can be guilty, in the opinion of the highest cultures it is the proper occupation of man.

It is not for me to suggest the times and places when this can be done. I have no wish to draw up rules, nor do I think of spirituality as a matter of rules. For some, perhaps the clergy, it will be the proper occupation of the hour before or after breakfast; for others, the laity, it might well be the last half-hour in the arm-chair before going to bed, or the lunch-hour, or the time spent in travelling. The time must be the choice of those who know the circumstances of their own life. All I do know is that there must be time if there is to be any meaning or conveying of reality in the rest of life.

The In-Christ Involvement in Life

The Lord's Prayer is the prototype of our Christian spirituality: first perspective, then action. In time there will be need to be the standing back for reflection on the perspectives of ourselves and our life, and the going forward in-Christ into the world, but it is a great mistake to call the first prayer the second action. Both are prayer: prayer is the interaction of thought and involvement. Spirituality is the whole activity of living: it is the total response to our existence seen from the point of view of what life is leading to. But what is effective prayer-love in action? How do we see Christ under the species of our daily bread, and meet him where he encounters us in the world? The Bishop of Woolwich says:

> Prayer is the responsibility to meet others with all that I have, to be ready to encounter the unconditional in the conditional, to expect to meet God in the way, not to turn aside from the way. (*Honest to God*, p. 100)

But what does this mean in terms of the approach I make to life? How do we spell out this in-Christ relationship to life? We have tried to do this by set times and set words which we call prayer, but, as Macleod says, it is not the intention that is wrong but the method—the set words, places and times become dead because the pressures of life in which they have become meaningful are not with us at the times we have called prayer. But if this is not the method, then what is? That is the question which on all sides we are being asked to spell out in terms which are communicable and relevant to modern man.

I believe that the tests which we can apply to our daily actions to see whether they are or are not actions of a living spirituality, of a prayer-love in action, of an in-Christness in the world, are threefold: first, by the way we approach the world itself and life itself; secondly, by the way we approach people; thirdly, by the conscious motivation of what we are doing. Again, notice how these three ways approximate closely to the Lord's Prayer: life—the daily bread; people—acceptance; motive—lead and deliver. Let me now, therefore, try to show in practical terms what this kind of prayer-living will look like.

(1) *The way we approach the world and life*

All too often the Church has seemed to set in opposition the world and God, the flesh and the spirit. We have had a defective spirituality because we have had a defective theology about the world and the flesh: to hate and flee the world is Jansenism: to call the flesh evil is Manicheism, and both these are officially heresies but all too often our whole attitude has been the attitude ofthe heresy.

The true Incarnational approach to life has been summed up admirably in an excellent article in *The Way* (a Roman Catholic Review of Spirituality) on *The Worldly Christian* by Fr. Oliver Ellis:

> The Word was made flesh and was in the midst of us as one who serves. It is within this world that man has his meaning, his activity has entered the economy of grace. Matter can never lose its dignity since its assumption into divinity, nor human nature since its divinization in the person of the Word. Life or happiness or progress are not unimportant. If we seek first the kingdom of God all these will be added to us. A fascinating vista opens up, a theology and spirituality of history, of the human situation, a sense of purpose forward-looking and dynamic enough to outdazzle Marxian messianism: Christian enthusiasm for the conquering of pain and hunger and distance and the fatigue of work, and the limitless possibilities for the evolution of humanity. The world is sick for the Church, said Hadrian the Seventh, but the world will not confess it as long as the Church poses as her rival. (*The Way*, Vol. 6, No. 1)

In these words is summed up the approach which we make as we go in-Christ into the world: we shall rejoice in its secularity, in its desire for the increasing maturity of man, in its scientific progress; we shall unite ourselves with the increasing unity of all things, whether it be the unity of the unfolding knowledge of the universe, the unity of all Christians, the unity of men in peace and justice. We shall not see the world as a challenge to our Christian living: we shall not want to run away from it into some kind of Christian ghetto. We shall want to listen to the voice of the world in the kind of thinking which is going on; we shall read the novels of Camus, the plays of Osborne, Pinter, Becket, and Ionesco, so that we may see how God is at work in those who are striving to find meaning and purpose in living, in those who are (albeit as conscious agnostics) rejoicing in the maturity and the strength of man and sorrowing for the absurdity and the lack of meaning for man. We shall feel within us the desire to praise God for His world by rejoicing in it and having hope for it: indeed it will be this sense of rejoicing and hope which will be our act of praise: our seeing in the midst of life today the Word made flesh and made flesh through us.

It is this kind of optimistic approach, not the facile optimism of the old-fashioned liberal modernist, but the approach of belief in what man is doing through science and technology and seeing in this the working of God, "hidden", as it were, in the evolutionary processes of man the Christ moving in the hearts of men and in their corporate lives, which marks the great appeal for many a modern man of the works of Teilhard de Chardin. He himself once said: "Marxists *believe* in the future of mankind while present-day Christians do not." The approach to life of a true involvement spirituality will be an approach which believes in the future of mankind because Christ is in that future. The Christian who can interpret theologically both the world of to-day and the world of tomorrow will be providing the best kind of answer to what often seem the despairs of the modern writers and the pointlessness of much modern humanism.

A truly incarnational approach will also rejoice in the flesh of man, if I may use that word to indicate all that goes with the joy of physical living. Bonhoeffer spoke of the need to be with man in his strength, in his joy, in the fullness of his living, and I do not think Christian spirituality has spoken enough to man in his joys, the joys of his senses as well as the joys of his spirit. We have often only seemed able to speak to man in his sorrows and in what Bonhoeffer calls the "gaps" of his life. To be able to appreciate and understand good food, good wine, good company, is to have the Christ of the wedding-feast with us. To be able to be in-Christ in the sexual act would take away much of the ghastly dualism of flesh and spirit which has bedevilled Christian thinking about sexuality. In perhaps no respect more than in this realm has the fatal influence of Manicheism been evident. In my last book, *No New Morality*, I quoted Sherwin Bailey as saying:

> The general impression left by the Church's teaching upon simple and unlearned people can only have been that the physical relationship of the sexes was regarded by religion as unworthy, if not shameless and obscene.

An interesting example of this is the lack of much Christian writing or much Christian prayer on the *joy* of sexuality; I once tried in vain to find any prayer in books of prayers which either thanked God for the gift of sex or for the gift of wine or for the gift of holidays or dancing. But why not? If we can happily thank God publicly for the gift of food and sleep, why not for the other great gift of physical living? Solovyev, the Russian theologian, in *The Meaning of Love*, says that the sexual act in love is perhaps the nearest human thing to the life which has understood what real unification with God in love means because it is the human parallel to the real giving and unity which expresses itself in participation. Let every sexual act, then, be an act of prayer and we shall gain a more healthy view of sexuality, see more clearly what God made flesh means, and realize that sex without love is sex without Christ.

But just because a truly incarnational approach to life believes in the future of mankind and rejoices in the joys of men, it will also be concerned for those things which mar that future and for those men who are deprived of the joys of life. To pray for daily bread is to work for the needs we know in the brother we know. Our Lord brings out this aspect of involvement spirituality in the story of the Good Samaritan. Here are three people, the priest, the Levite and the Samaritan; the first two were undoubtedly men of prayer but they had never understood that prayer means involvement and not set forms of words. They did not see in helping the wounded man the very prayer to which God was calling them. The Samaritan saw that it was just as he opened his heart in compassion to the wounded man that he let the love of God in and so brought into his action that in-Christness which is the heart of prayer. The Parable of the Sheep and the Goats also brings home forcibly to us that it is our recognition of the presence of Christ in those who need Him that constitutes our spirituality, and not the words we use and the professions we make.

The first necessity then of our in-Christ involvement in life is to find within us, or to train ourselves to find, the proper emotions and feelings for the world in which we live so that we may recognize where God is at work and where He is not, and unite ourselves with Him in His redemption of the world. This will mean a *belief* in the hopes and skills and progress of modern man, a *rejoicing* in the *whole* life of man, physical, mental and spiritual, and a *concern* which is seen in practical effort for the needs of men.

(2) *The way we approach people*

The second evidence of a living spirituality will be by the way we approach people.

> To open oneself to another unconditionally in love is to be with him in the presence of God and that is the heart of intercession. To pray for another is to expose both oneself and him to the common ground of our being: it is to see one's concern for him in terms of ultimate concern, to let God into the relationship. Intercession is to be with another at that depth whether in silence or compassion or action. (*Honest to God*, p. 100)

What then is this meeting with Christ in that man? It is surely the meeting of the Christ in me with the Christ in him and that is to be at prayer with him in the meeting; for the meeting is "I-in-Christ—thou-in-Christ". To be with him is to be in the love which casts out fear and insecurity, which makes possible total self-giving with neither fear nor seeking for rewards. And relationships in Christ are deeper than any merely human relationships can be because they are in perfect love (which no human relationship *per se* achieved). One might say that to be in Christ with another is the depth of our humanity since He is the perfect man.

What then will be the characteristics of this in-Christ relationship with people? The relationships of Christ in His earthly life will show us. They will be first complete and unreserved acceptance and openness; secondly, the willingness to give them the significance which is their right and to help them to deeper knowledge of themselves; thirdly, to bring them to the demands of maturity and responsibility which are within the realities of their situation. I would now spell out in greater detail what this approach to people means.

(a) *Complete and unreserved acceptance and openness*

Christ found himself constantly in the company of publicans and sinners and they felt at home with him. Why? Because they were accepted, they were made to feel that the condition of being publicans and sinners is simply the condition of every man and the love of God is not confined to those who have established themselves in their own views of righteousness. I, therefore, conscious of my own acceptance without desert by Christ, go into the world without the necessity to demand certain standards from others before I can accept them. Yet this is so often what we do. So often our concern for the deprived and the outcast is limited to words rather than to actions; we are prepared to sympathize so long as we may do it at a distance but not if it involves bringing them right into the sphere of our personal and family life. We excuse ourselves from too close concern by saying that this is a matter for the specialist, yet in fact often what is really needed in prayer-love in action is not some specialist concern, treating the publican and sinner however well as a case-study, but simply someone who cares. This is surely the greatest example of intercession-living there can be. Another article in *The Way* by Mr Hugh Kay puts this better than I could myself:

> I know of a man, recently freed after a prison sentence for offences against small children: suffering from a heart affliction that makes it unsafe for him to work near machinery; living on national assistance in a single, very seedy room. He is unloved and unlovable and Christ died for him. Somehow in him we have to see the Spirit of Christ struggling for self-assertion and recognition. Admit the unbalanced or the grievously erring to your fireside? bring him within the orbit of your innocent children? put up with his everlasting harping on his own feelings? forgive him repeatedly when he steals from you and insults you and asks to be taken back? someone, somewhere seems to answer with another question: are these things, or are they not, the concern of the life of the Spirit? (*The Way*, Vol. 6, No. 3, p. 216)

I would give a personal illustration of the same nature. I was once asked to go and minister to a man who had just been arrested for raping a thirteen-month-old baby. I was filled with such repulsion for the act that I knew it was useless for me to go just like that. Before I could be of any use to him I had to learn to accept him: this was a task for me. If I had gone then and there I would have carried nothing of Christ, only one human being feeling repulsion for another—which repulsion would have been sensed. That I might be in true prayer-relationship with him I had first to work this repulsion out of my own system, I had to let the spirit of Christ work within me. Then and then only could I go, and when I went I saw such a wretched and tortured human being who had so far gone from the reality of his true self that nothing but the reality of God struggling through me and through him mattered. I was with him in the ground of both of our beings: we were at prayer and the result of that relationship did as much for me as for him.

But it is not only the approach to the unfortunate and to the misfits but also the ordinary every-day approach to people which will show whether or not I have a living spirituality in my approach. The humanity of Jesus was and is a humanity which dares to be itself in complete openness to other people: He had the "courage to be". Never in the whole course of the Gospel story do we get the impression of one who was putting on an act, adopting a pose, trying to live up to other people's expectations of Him. He was at home in the most amazing diversity of surroundings because he was just Himself. He played no role, He had no self for one situation, and another self for another situation. He did not see people as "contacts" to be used; He did not try to possess or to smother people with His emotions; He did not fail to distinguish one person from another and did not lump people into a group; He did not love them for what they might become. He was neither solemn nor superficial; he cared nothing for class distinctions or accents; he was not impressed by power and worldly position. He was capable of irony, laughter and tears. He could be angry; shrink naturally from pain ("If it be thy will, take this cup from me"); He could be very outspoken and even, sometimes, contemptuous ("Go and tell that fox" (Herod)); he never compromised. In one thing He was utterly consistent: He was always true to the truth He proclaimed for He had made that truth His own in His own living and experience. He lived by the love He proclaimed and that love was, as it always is, both reconciling and divisive. It attracted both love and hostility as love will always attract. It meant just as much the resolute opposition to the evil and destructive in humanity as the encouragement and seeing what is creative and good in humanity. In one sense He was always an outsider to the world, in another He was the worldly man *par excellence*. He was born and died an outsider: born outside the normal conventions of child-birth—"no room at the inn", died outside the normal conventions of decent dying—on a cross outside the city walls; he never conformed to the world's expectation—He did not stick close to His family, He did not observe his position in society, He lived a rather beatnik sort of life with no settled home, accepting hospitality where He could get it with graciousness and naturalness, in no way feeling under any obligation to those who gave it. He had no hesitation in challenging those in authority, He was very careless of those with whom He associated, He had no worry about His reputation when an ex-tart joined His followers, nor did it worry Him that people might think He was homosexual by going round with a group of men and letting John lean on His breast at supper. In all these ways He was an outsider. But yet He was at home with all men: at the age of twelve He could mix naturally in the temple with a group of scholars; He could equally accept the hospitality of Simon the Pharisee, of Zacchaeus the publican; He could promote the gaiety of a wedding by providing extra wine when they had already well drunk; He could share the feelings of Martha and Mary when their brother had died: He could give great gifts of healing to the twisted spirits crying out for integration; He could receive without embarrassment gifts for Himself of costly ointment to cleanse His road-dusty feet. He could speak naturally to complete strangers without having to be introduced; He could be at home with fishermen, tax-collectors, tarts, learned men, scribes, religious leaders, Jews and Romans. He could speak with dignity and on equal terms without arrogance to the High Priest and to the Roman Governor; He could afford to ignore with dignity King Herod. He could speak with equal love on the Cross to soldiers, to a dying criminal, to those who jeered at Him, as to His Mother and His best friend: yet that same love could be sufficiently detached to enable Him without compunction to leave his home and family and to make no distinction within the group of disciples between those He felt special affection for on closer intimate terms and the others.

(b) *Significance and self-awareness*

This then is the in-Christ relationship with others which must be ours if we are to carry into life a prayer-relationship: what Christ was then He is now in us. As Bonhoeffer said, the Christian is the worldly man *par excellence*, but he is also the outsider. He carries within him the tensions, the strains, the stresses, the joys, the successes of the world in which he lives. He has understood that the Christian God, unlike all others, dares to be human. We shall then approach people with both that set apartness from the world which refuses to be bound by the world's conventions and distinctions, and that love of the world which sees all men as in Christ and their significance as the significance which is his in them. We shall challenge the divisions and roles of society, whether within or without the Church; we shall refuse to put Christ into the strait-jacket of a Church with preconceived moral judgements. (What a pity it was that Billy Graham chose to make a solemn descent on Soho, having described it as a square mile of sin—how much more effective if such a descent had been made on Surbiton or Purley! Could there not have been a wry smile on the face of Christ at the girl who danced on the top of Billy Graham's car, thus making her protest at the God who descended on her rather than being involved in loving relationship with her!) We shall equally refuse to be so interested in the outsider that we have no room or interest for perhaps the rather ordinary, dull (or so it seems to us) person who leads a normal conventional life. I remember how I, as a parish priest, used often to forget the names of certain middle-aged ladies in the parish. This was significant: I was not interested in them. People only look alike when there is no love.

We must equally learn the Benedicite:

O ye murderers and thieves,
O ye delinquents and tarts,
O ye alcoholics and drug-addicts,
O ye homosexuals and lesbians,
  Bless ye the Lord;

as the Benedicite:

O ye status-seekers and affluent,
O ye conventional and respectable,
O ye frustrated spinsters and possessive mothers,
O ye complacent and disapproving,
  Bless ye the Lord.

Christ in us knows both the loneliness of the outsider and the crabbed lives of the insider. He experiences in us the full diversity of the human condition. The meeting of the Christ in us with the Christ in others will mean that we shall be willing to expose ourselves in openness to others without fear, seeing each person we meet as having a significance because both of us are accepted and loved by God.

> I can only acknowledge the unconditional significance of another person or believe in him (without which true love is impossible) by affirming him in God, and therefore by belief in God himself, and in myself, as possessing in God the centre and root of my existence. (Vladimir Soloviev, *The Meaning of Love*, p. 59)

To have a prayerful approach to people is to have eyes to see, a mind intent upon seeing, a heart hopeful of seeing the image of God in each person I meet, to see them in themselves and in God.

It is only when this significance has been given by us in our approach to people, when we have freed ourselves of the need to assess blame and responsibilities, that we can take them on to the next step on the road to redemption, namely, to be aware of their true selves and that which is blocking the potentialities which lie within them. It is this kind of freedom which the Christ in us brings in our personal approach: the Christ who revealed to the Samaritan woman the truths she was concealing from herself, who enabled the blind man not only to see physically but to seespiritually, who enabled the prostitute to realize the real love which lay within her. As I said in my previous book:

> He is constantly opening the eyes of people to a reality greater than is at present known to them, so that they may surrender what they imagine or hope or fear they are to what in fullness they really are: so that they may not be guilty about themselves or hide themselves, but be themselves and love themselves. (*No New Morality*, p. 26)

This will mean that in our encounters with people we shall do a great deal of listening in order that we may learn how people do see themselves. By sensitivity to what is heard, and by insight into the right kind of questions to be put, we may be able both to build up the fearful and insecure and rightly disturb and undermine the complacent—those who are "too much at ease in Zion".

(c) *Demands of maturity and responsibility*

Christ calls us to know ourselves so that by true love of ourselves we may learn what it means to have love towards our neighbour, to have a right sense of responsibility and maturity in our relationships with others. This also then will be our in-Christ relationship with others. Christian love is not soft: it is very demanding, but it is not the demand of slavish obedience to a set of rules worked out in advance and imposed upon others. Rather is it the working out with others as fellow-travellers along the road of life what is the appropriate responsibility within the given situation: to learn to help each other ask the right questions before we try to find the right answers. Effective prayer-love in action means effective intercession in action. Intercession in action means the realization of inter-relationship in all fields of life and the responsibilities which go with that realization.

There are two important points to remember in helping people to the demands of a mature responsibility: the first is that Christ did not impose laws to which all had to conform, but He dealt with people where they were and led them on to the next stage of where they could be. He will not ask of them what they cannot attain as yet, and He will not ask of them what is not in them. Secondly, He dealt with them in the realities of the situation where they were and not in some ideal plane where they were not. So in our encounters with others: we go into the world to meet people and we know that our true responsibility towards them in that meeting is to help them both to see and to do what is the most responsible and loving thing in the given situation, not to hold up before them and pressurize them into some ideal which cannot be actualized as a basis of conduct. This is to deal, not with mature responsibility, but with make-believe fantasy. (See in this connection my own arcticle in *The New Christian* (May 5, 1966). Nicolas Berdyaev said:

> Every moral action should have in view a concrete living person and not the abstract good.

The questions we shall help them to answer because they are ours as well are: What is the action *I* must take? What effects will this have on others also involved? Can I take the action I know I should? What shall I have to face and deal with in myself first? What are the limits of the best action that can be taken? What are the possibilities and alternatives within the situation? What are the likely consequences of these alternatives? This is how petition and intercession arise in action out of the context of living relationship with others.

(3) *The conscious motivation of what we are doing*

The third test which we apply to see whether our daily involvements are reflections of a living spirituality, an in-Christ prayer-life relationship, is the test of the conscious motivation of what we are doing. The third part of the Lord's Prayer is such conscious motivation: it asks for leadership and deliverance. The essence of a relevant spirituality, as I have said in many different ways, is the sense of the God in the here and now of life. That is why the last section will have puzzled many because they will say, "But what you have been talking about isn't *praying*, it is *living*." May I repeat again: praying is living, but it is living with a conscious motivation and purpose, and if we do not have this conscious motivation we are apt simply to be a good humanist, an activist of good works. On a previous page I quoted a rather strange conversation between a Zen Buddhist monk and a business man. The monk is trying to show the business man that it is in our everyday thoughts, in our "walking on" in life, our "yes" to life, that we are praying; that this is done among the chairs, the tables, the trays, the fireplaces and the windows. This is true, but for most of us there will need to be constant reminders of this truth, sometimes by the deliberate recollection in the midst of involvement of why we are doing what we are doing; sometimes by an ejaculation, utterance or gesture which, like the bread and wine at Communion, is a visible reminder that "whatever wakes my heart or mind thy presence is, my Lord".

It is this conscious motivation which distinguishes the Christian from the humanist. We often in our daily living may not *do* things differently from the non-Christian, but I think we shall do them from a different motivation and purpose: we may simply be seen, to use the Bishop of Woolwich's terminology, as the gracious neighbour; but we shall desire, and rightly desire, that the seeing of the gracious neighbour does lead to the seeing of the gracious God and does not just stop at ourselves, but to the Christ in ourselves. The motivation and purpose of our doing is expressed by St Paul: "And whatever you do, in word or deed, do everything in the name of the Lord, giving thanks to God the Father through him" (Colossians 3: 17).

How, then, shall we remind ourselves of this motivation, be conscious of the Christ in us speaking and acting towards the Christ in others? The first way is by sincerity. Does what we really want in life conform to what we profess to want? There is a terrible phrase in the Psalms, "Thou gavest them their heart's desires and sent leanness withal into their souls". So often that is exactly what happens; we are given not what we profess, but what we really want, and this crabs and confines our life because our real wants fall short of the stature of the fullness of Christ. John Burnaby writes:

> We may not approach God with a feigned devotion fearing to tell him what we really want. If I am to learn what God wants, the way to it is not to disown the inmost desires of my heart but rather deliberately to spread them out before the Lord—to face with all the honesty I can achieve the real truth about my desires, to wrestle with the sham of professing desires which are not really mine. The schooling of desires is indeed prayer. (*Soundings*, p. 235)

At one time there was a difficult member of our Cathedral Chapter whose persistence in putting forward his own point of view was such that it seemed one had to choose between capitulation and long and exhaustive argument. I often used to find that at the Eucharist prior to the Chapter meeting my mouth was praying for harmony and agreement at the meeting but my heart was saying "I hope that this time we can successfully sit upon X." It is not surprising that the results of the Chapter meetings were a very painful schooling of desire!

Secondly, it will mean that the whole of life will be approached consciously with confession, thanksgiving, adoration: confession for all that in me is not wanting to be in Christ, that would desire Christ to be elsewhere; thanksgiving for the glory, the strength, the beauty, the pain—for all that is Christ in me, my true authentic self, meeting all that is Christ in another, his true authentic self; adoration—to want Christ to be where one is. This is to make confession, thanksgiving and adoration what they should be: not forms of words, but willed attitudes to living: to will that this dance of life which is Christ's (as the song puts it) may be the one in which daily he leads us:

> Dance then wherever you may be
> I am the lord of the dance, said he,
> And I'll lead you all wherever you may be
> I'll lead you all in the dance, said he.
>
> (Sydney Carter)

Thirdly, it will mean that we shall not scorn the little arrows of ejaculatory thought which are often called arrow prayers for they are the in-Christ gestures which He Himself in his Incarnation frequently made, e.g. "he looked up", "he blessed". Such are the "Prayer of Jesus" developed first in the East, mentioned by Salinger in one of his novels where the perpetually repeated formula of "Lord Jesus, have mercy on me" was based upon the idea of making Christ the whole of our thought and our life, as the act of breathing is the accompaniment of living; the "God bless this man" sitting next to me in the bus or the underground, which brings me into conscious relationship in Christ with one with whom I do not and at that moment cannot have any other involvement relationship; the Sign of the Cross or "Jesus, help," which can be willed coming into His presence at a time of sudden temptation or sudden difficulty and can effectively disperse both the temptation and the feeling that everything is on top of one. All these are but realizations that expressions in very brief words or signs in a sensory world are sensory or visual reminders of the living Christ forcing His way through us: they are not talking to God, they are but the visual or ejaculatory signs of His presence amongst us as the day's engagements take their toll of glory and shame.

These, then, are the ways of that involvement in Christ in life which is the second part of prayer living: by the way I approach life, the way I approach people and the conscious motivation of all that I do, I am realizing the Christ-in-me, Christ-in-the-other, Christ-in-the-midst, which is the very heart and meaning of prayer in action.

A Relevant Modern Asceticism

I said earlier that asceticism is the recognition of the cost of Christian love. There are some expressions of love which cannot be made without fasting and mortification. The questions we have to ask ourselves are: What is a modern approach to asceticism? How does asceticism itself become a matter not of law but of love? There have been two dangers to traditional asceticism: the first is that so often it has become a matter of the observance of inward-looking and rather petty laws which bear far more resemblance to the deadly codes of the Pharisees than to the costliness of the Cross. I find it very difficult to understand what purpose of love towards God or neighbour is served by this kind of asceticism: I see a very great resemblance between this and the nagging which went on constantly by the Pharisees towards Our Lord's actions on the Sabbath, but I had thought in my innocence that this kind of Pharisaism was not an act of love towards Our Lord but was strongly rebuked by Him!

I often feel in the same way that the penances imposed at Confession seem to make nonsense of the word "penance". If they are symbolic, as I have often been told, because there is no real penance that can be made, then let us not have "pretend" penances; let us openly admit that no real penance can be made.

Again, so often what happens in Lent has more of the nature of self-imposed masochism which is a perversion rather than a virtue.

If these are dangers of trying to follow rules, there are more serious dangers in the kind of asceticism which arises from a hatred of the flesh or of the world. Such asceticisms have led to the perverted view of sexuality of which I spoke earlier—of marriage as a lower order of living than celibacy—or to such rules as abstinence from conjugal relationships during Lent or on vigils, which is to take over directly the old Jewish view that there was something tainted about sex so that the men could not eat the holy bread unless they had abstained from women. Such a view of the flesh has led to the belief that the taking of wine or any kind of alcoholic drink is sinful and, in the extreme case of the Brethren, to a rigid apartheid in which one cannot even take food with an "unbeliever". It is very interesting and rather ironic that with the more Evangelical kind of Protestant it is only some aspects of the world that are sinful: it will be sinful to play cricket on Sundays but not to eat a large dinner and then go to sleep in the armchair; it will be sinful to go to the theatre, the cinema, the pub, but it will not be sinful to make money, to involve oneself in the commercial world, to reap quite considerable rewards and live by quite comfortable standards!

However, let us now leave the negative side of what is not a relevant asceticism for today and turn to what is. I would say that there are two aspects of a relevant asceticism for today: one is that it should be an asceticism related to life, a life which is understood as a willed expression of the love of God and a consequent serving love for one's neighbour, so that the ascetical practices will be not for the abnegation of life and the crushing of love but rather at the service of life and springing from a love of life as the great sphere of the work of God's creation. My critical self-discipline will then turn on the questions: Am I talking of love or willing to bear the pain of love? Am I really being open to the demands of God and my fellow-men? The other aspect of a relevant asceticism is that it should be concerned with the resistance of those pressures of the world upon myself which are liable to lead me away from what is creative and towards what is destructive both for myself and for others, which is ready to suffer for truth in the midst of falsehood, which is ready to fight against the self-destructiveness of the world, against the insidious pressures of environment and society in order that the true meaning of God's created reality may be revealed. In other words, a true asceticism results both from a love of and openness to the world, to all the creative joy of the Resurrection life in the world, which is through and not by-passing the Crucified life in the world, and also a renunciation of the world, a renunciation of all that is unreal to the true glory and unifying creativity of the world. It will mean asking questions such as: What is poverty? What is obedience? What is chastity today?

Let me now try to give illustrations of both these kinds of asceticisms:

(a) *An asceticism which is related to life open to love of God and of neighbour*

This is put for us strongly by Isaiah: "Is it such a fast that I have chosen? a day for a man to afflict his soul . . . Is not this the fast that I have chosen? to loosen the bands of wickedness, to undo the heavy burdens . . . Is it not to deal thy bread to the hungry, and that thou bring the poor that are cast out to thy house?" (Isa. 58: 5–7) and of course this is echoed in the Parable of the Sheep and the Goats and in St Paul's words about he that has abundance supplying the need of those who have not. The asceticism which is really concerned with the love of God and with the needs of men will be costly because it will want to identify with those in whom the Cross of Christ is being expressed—if the Christ-in-me is to meet the Christ-in-the-other, then also the crucified Christ in me will meet the crucified Christ in the other. Self-giving to the utmost is being crucified with Christ. It may mean giving everything away—even our own righteousness, even our own worship. Such a relevant asceticism will be tied to no programme and to no rules: it will arise out of the situation when within the situation is the consciously motivated desire to bring Christ into it. I can think of many ways in which such an asceticism might be worked out: the going for a whole day without food that the pangs of hunger may be really felt (as they are not after missing one meal) might identify the Christ in the starving Indian with the Christ in the starving me; the refusal to be "choosy" about food (a very real sin of gluttony is the delicate "picking and choosing" of what I will and will not eat—much more a sin of youth than many of the so-called sins).

Another form of asceticism which might well apply in an age of scarce housing and many homeless might be the deliberate refusal to live in a large house which one could afford and instead have that house converted into flats for those who need homes, retaining only what is necessary for oneself and family: by this means there is identification with need.

A different kind of asceticism within the religious sphere will be the willingness to forgo forms of worship with which one has grown up and to which one has become devoted, in order that worship might become relevant to others outside the Church or to suit the needs of a changing community structure. The Anglo-Catholic and Evangelical, instead of fighting to the last ditch to retain what is convenient and desirable to them, might have a disciplined asceticism which is capable of seeing the wider needs of the Church and realizing that unity is more important than a clinging to past traditions which all too often rationalize "what I want" into "what is true". It might even sometimes be necessary to forgo the act of worship itself if someone really needs you at that moment, or if your place of involvement is the Trades Union meeting which is called on a Sunday morning.

There is also the asceticism which is deliberately undertaken to test the sincerity and concern of what we are doing: "this kind cometh not out, save by prayer and fasting". I remember once being asked to lay hands upon a lady for whom the doctors had given up hope and who was in a state of constant depression and almost despair. I visited her and talked to her about this sacrament and I found that as a result she was filled with a great sense of expectation and hope in the awaiting of my coming to anoint and lay hands. Such was my faithlessness that I was tormented with the fear that nothing would happen and that her expectations would not be fulfilled and that this would plunge her into even greater despair. I was moved to study again that passage in which Our Lord dealt with the apostles whose efforts had proved fruitless: I read how he rebuked them and then said, "This kind cometh not out, save by prayer and fasting." I determined for the sake of this lady and the proof of my desire for her and test of faith, to fast for a whole day before laying on hands. When I came to the laying on of hands there was the reality of healing in the midst of us: the healing Christ in me meeting the healing Christ in her. She was not actually cured of the disease but never again did she have the extremity of pain and depression she had had before. The local doctor said to me: "Something has happened to Mrs X that I could never have done for her: it is as if despite the disease a wholeness has come to her." I mention this simply because this is the kind of asceticism I am sure that today needs, the kind reflected in Michel Quoist's prayer on *Hunger* and *Housing*. As Bouyer says:

> The purifying efficacy of the mortification of fasting and the impetus it gives to our prayer will be in function of the very concrete preoccupation with our neighbour and his needs that goes along with it. (*Introduction to Spirituality*, p. 180)

This then is one side of that asceticism which is openness to love of God and of neighbour: it will not consist in rather silly and formal rules about fasting for one hour before Communion or no sweets in Lent, nor will it be a gratuitous severity towards the flesh, which looks more like masochism than love. Rather will it be that understanding of the costliness of love which will have no standard pattern, but will take many forms arising out of the situation and its needs. It might be said that there is "situational asceticism" as well as "situational ethics" in a relevant spirituality today. It will be the task of a spiritual director or counsellor to help each individual to realize in what directions the costliness of love is leading them rather than to give a preformulated book of rules.

(b) *The resistance to the destructive pressures of the world*

The other aspect of asceticism very relevant to today is that mortification which is not viewed as a battle against the flesh on the mistaken assumption that the flesh is evil but rather as a struggle against a distorted and selfish view of life, where the true demands and the true values of life are being set aside for inferior demands and values, the struggle against a world that is not God's world but a world that has become God's enemy. Such asceticism will be a warfare against the insidious forces in the environment, which are hiding from us the reality of God and putting up unreal gods in His place. It will mean an assessment of what in the world of today the great virtues of poverty, obedience and chastity mean.

What then are the destructive pressures of today? Riesman, the sociologist, says that today there is an other-directedness which results in spiritual impoverishment, and by this he means that so many people live their lives on the expectations of their neighbours. Their values are determined by what other people think, by the conditioning forces of convention, or by the pressures of advertisement. Archbishop Ramsey says:

> There is a tendency for modern man to live in a whirl with his mind over-crowded. I sometimes think that an important part of our Christian asceticism needs to be the discipline of the mind to secure its freedom even more than the discipline of the body.

The chains from which God wishes modern man to be free are the chains of lust for things, pride in power and possessions. Resistance to advertisement pressures is surely one of the most important tasks of Christian asceticism today.

Poverty in the world of today means that we shall be freed from the inordinate love of possessions or the constant demand for security. We shall be capable of assessing our needs, not in terms of what our neighbour has or what the so-called standard of life of our class demands, but by sensitivity to the economic possibilities of the true welfare of our country and the world, by sensitivity to the claims of other people, by recognition of the true worth of things. We shall see things not simply as a means to an end but as a gift of God with, therefore, the necessary exercise of possessions as the exercise of our own stewardship of those gifts as servants of God. A Roman Catholic expert on moral theology, Fr Haring, writes:

> By poverty we mean to be able to acquire, not without struggle against selfishness, a purified love of all values and earthly realities. The man who is poor in spirit rejects the use of things simply as a means. He recognizes in them the gift of God. He perceives in them the call of God. He is able to appreciate their true worth, for he sees them as a sign of the love of his heavenly father. But because of this he understands as well that he is challenged to give them up or modify his use of them whenever the needs of his fellow men demand it. (Bernard Haring, C.SS.R: *A Modern Approach to the Ascetical Life* in *Worship*, Vol. 39, No. 10)

Obedience in the world of today means an in-Christ obedience to the understanding and working out of Christian insights and values in the worldly involvements of life, so that our obedience is not pressurized by society's conventions and worldly estimates of what is success: it is the bringing to bear of what St Paul calls the "foolishness of God" upon the wisdom of the world: "If any man among you seemeth to be wise in this world let him become a fool that he may be wise" (1 Cor. 3: 18). Obedience to the will of God in worldly affairs will often seem to be foolishness because it will take little account of status symbols, power blocs, the worth of man in terms of money and position (all things which an other-directed society holds dear). Our ascetical obedience will be to train ourselves to make the kind of judgements that God makes, not the kind of judgement that society makes.

Chastity in the modern world will bear no resemblance to some technical definition as to whether or not one has had sexual relationship to the point of coitus. Rather will it be the understanding of what kind of self-control is needed in order that people may behave towards each other as mature men and women: it will be the realization that people are people of minds, spirits and bodies and that all three enter into every relationship. Chastity will mean that the gods of pressurization, which are strongest of all in the world of sexuality, will be resisted tooth and nail, but not in the interests of a false prudery but in the interests of "growing up" into maturity. The childishness of the advertisement which will try to say that the only important factor in personal relationship is something called "glamour" (hence the pressurization on cosmetics and sweet smells for both men and women) which anyway dies completely somewhere round about the age of forty; the fake values of the Girl goddess who is worshipped through beauty contests as a standardized and statisticized symbol of a world which has lost the understanding of what real beauty is; the vicious attacks on sex made by *Playboy*, where all the joy of sexuality is taken away in a pseudo-Puritan attempt to relegate sex to casual encounter and the woman to a plaything (afterwards to be discarded) of the man—all these are the enemies of chastity today, because they are the enemies of what is real and beautiful in personal relationship and what is mature in human behaviour. The ascetical pursuit of chastity will be the pursuit of that freedom found in Christ which enables us to be real in our relationships with others.

Group Spirituality

The fourth requirement of a relevant spirituality is the modern equivalent of the religious community. It is rapidly becoming apparent that within the life of the Church the working out of things through the small group has become the norm of approach. These groups, where there is opportunity for both listening and contributing, bridge the gap between the "personal" spirituality of the individual and the corporate act of worship; they enable the kind of acceptance necessary in an in-Christ approach to people and the kind of understanding of what worldly involvement means and its costliness, which can come through a pooling of experience and the discussion of common concerns in an atmosphere of common trust.

What is characteristic of modern society is becoming equally characteristic of modern spirituality within the life of the Church, namely the need to draw together with our peers to work together on problems in teams, to experience a common solidarity o obviate the dread of loneliness. Usually the whole congregation of a Church is too large to enable such a common sharing, understanding and acceptance to take place, and yet the whole tendency of the newly awakened consciousness of the role of the laity does not allow that all matters of spirituality shall depend upon the clergy, however "holy" they may be. How then will such groups work within the realm of spirituality? Usually they will consist of about eight to twelve people meeting together in each other's houses for the discussion of common problems, either of their work or of their neighbourhood life, and trying to relate their Christian insights to the shared knowledge of the complexities and pressures of their daily work and life. Sometimes the initiative for such group life will come from a week-end spent away together at some Conference House to thresh out the relationship of faith and life through Biblical study linked to case-study. Such are the kind of training week-ends which the Parish Life Conference initiates in many dioceses. These week-ends (which we in Southwark have been running for the past four years) usually end with the group discovering not only the complexity of in-Christ involvement in the world, but also their own inadequacies for meeting such involvement and their own need for continued meeting to find their spiritual guidance from each other. After all it is managers, social workers, housewives, teachers, who can best speak to one another and wrestle out what it means to be a Christian within their sphere of occupation. This is not something a clergyman can do for them, nor can they find sufficient experience to be able to do it personally without some sharing with those of similar experience.

As a result of such discussion together the group will not only learn the better what is Christian involvement in life, but will also learn much about human acceptance and the difficulties as well as the joys of community living: they will be able in discussion to observe each other's behaviour, especially if there has been some training in group dynamics, to realize how much we need to discipline ourselves to avoid domination or to encourage someone who finds it difficult to contribute, to be able to live with the tensions and resolve them, not avoid them.

Out of such group life there may well emerge various forms of group contemplation, or group vocal expression of its needs in the form of biddings to reflective thinking, or group concern expressed through the holding before the group by name of people with whom they are involved. I do not know, for example, why in the modern world a Retreat need be a time when the laity sit at the feet of some "holy" clergyman. It would be equally appropriate that the laity should conduct retreats for the clergy, or better still and likelier, that a retreat for laymen would be a mixed time of in-Christ motivated discussion followed by in-Christ motivated silent reflection upon what had been discussed. A highly successful Youth Retreat of this kind was held at Wychcroft last year when a group of young people met in small groups for discussion, then in the same groups spent time in silent reflection with, from time to time as guided by the Spirit, someone moved to express in words within the group the pattern of the reflection as it had come to him. This, of course, is no new experience for the Quakers but has a relevance and validity for all Christians today.

Out of such group thinking there might also emerge consideration of relevant patterns of spirituality for the corporate worship of the Church: one such group I know drew up with the clergy the kind of Lent course which they felt met their needs; another group let their own thinking be expressed in a short address given by one member expressing the thought of the group at the following Sunday Eucharist; another group helped the clergy to plan their next six months course of sermons.

There are many ways in which such a group spirituality may be expressed. What is important for our consideration of a relevant spirituality is to realize how such group life not only helps the laity and the clergy to the shared communal understanding of their in-Christ involvement with the world, but also provides them with reflective thinking which penetrates through what is unreal to what is real by the breaking down of facades within the group. Such a group-spirituality speaks to the need to express meaning within the involvements of daily life, and how to relate that meaning to corporate worship: it makes possible the kind of shared life and relationships which an impersonal society so much needs and which religious community in every age has provided, and it enables shared thinking which can be continued in the individual's own reflections in his time of personal contemplation.

These, then, are the various ways in which the fourfold needs of contemporary spirituality will be worked out. Two things now remain for our consideration: first, the kind of training which will be needed for such an understanding of spirituality, to which our last section naturally leads us because such training will obviously be mainly through small groups; secondly, the relationship of personal spirituality to the corporate spirituality expressed through public worship and what this will mean in our liturgical thinking and planning today.

CHAPTER 8

TRAINING IN PRAYING MY LIFE

I hope that it will be clearly seen that the whole concept of prayer of which I am speaking gets right away from the idea of prayer as speaking to another person apart from and invisible to the person engaged in living out the in-Christ life. Rather do I see prayer as the in-Christness which lights up all our actions in daily living from within. Training in the kind of spirituality of which I have been speaking will, therefore, start from *experience* both of myself and of the situation in which I find myself. I shall need, if I am to pierce through the shams and unrealities of life to the reality which lies beneath, to be trained to have the maximum capacity for true self-awareness, to know who I am and what I am. Self-awareness is not, however, something which is learnt in isolation but rather from relationship with others and in reaction to given situations. Therefore my training will be within my experience of a group and of the different relationships within different kinds of groups. It will really be a training in learning both to "love myself" and to "love my neighbour as myself." There will, however, always be a measurement by which I test the validity of my experiences and the group's experiences, and that measurement will be the full humanity of Christ which is to be expressed through me and recognized in others: "The mature manhood measured by the fullness of the stature of Christ" (Eph. 4: 13). This means that we shall have to be trained to recognize wherein lies maturity, for there is Christ both in us incognito and in others also incognito. This is what we mean by the prayer which is the conscious living with Christ, the ability to be able to recognize where Christ is and where Christ is not, and this has nothing to do with "churchiness", for often Christ is to be found in very non-religious settings and equally often is absent from the religious settings.

It will be through such personal experience, group experience, and capacity to recognize the in-Christness which is the measurement of His presence, that we shall learn how to reflect "as a man in his wholeness wholly attending", how to have an in-Christ involvement in life, what will be the asceticism which the costliness of that involvement brings, and what will be the nature of the religious community which supports us. There may well be words which will express all this in the verbalizing of our prayer but they will not be words addressed to a "thou" out there, but words which express the identification of God both with myself and with the situation, which express the experience of the recognition of where God is and where He is not. Let us now then begin to spell out the lines along which such training might be given.

First let me begin with the training of children. Here let us remember that the only way in which any experience of the presence of Christ can and will be given will be through the experience of trust, security, integrity and love in the human beings with whom the child is in contact. As the Newsom Report so wisely said:

> Teachers can only escape from their influence over the moral and spiritual development of their pupils by closing their schools. As long as they teach at all, whether they give formal lessons or not, they teach by the way they behave, by what they are. That is why one of the essential qualities of a teacher is integrity. (p. 53)

Mrs Robinson, writing in the Appendix to *The Honest to God Debate*, says much the same thing:

> The child will judge, love and assess how far he can trust from experience not only by the extent to which he can trust us and how far we trust him but also by his growing sense of a greater love in which both parents and child are grounded. Such an awareness can only be apprehended by the child from within. He learns it not from what we teach but from what we are.

I would think, therefore, that in the early days of childhood one does not teach a child to say his prayers but rather helps him to articulate the experiences which will be his from the experience of love in his parents and teachers. If we are providing a background of security in which a child can trust, we are expressing by what we are an experience of "underneath are the everlasting arms" of the one who is the ground of our being; if we are providing that kind of love in which the child finds freedom to express himself, freedom to rage without condemnation, freedom to show his needs and ask his questions without getting "fobbed off" or snubbed, then we are in fact presenting the love of Christ and the presence of Christ to a child whether or not it is at that stage understood as such. It will not be long in the lives of most children before they begin to ask the questions which reveal the early search for the understanding of the meaning of life. There will be that beginning of self-awareness which enables him to see that he is sometimes at odds with himself and with those whom he loves, and we shall have to help him understand what it is in him and in the situation which makes him feel like this: he begins to know when he has hurt someone by what he has done or said, and he will find out that forgiveness, reconciliation, sin are facts of his own understanding of himself. There will also be the beginning of the questions which concern themselves with the origin of things: "Where did I come from?" "What brought Mummy and Daddy together?" "Why does Grandpa have to die?" There will also be the beginning of understanding that life is a matter of community and that there are responsibilities to other members of the family: why things have to be shared with brothers and sisters, why there can only be good play with other children if each child is allowed reasonably equal participation.

It is when the questions start which arise from the experiences that there can then be put into words the articulation of the experience. The living Christ is the sign that the basis of all living from the infant at the breast to the end of life is love, and the capacity to love is a test of the progress we are making in life towards building a mature, well-integrated personality.

In the life of Christ is spelt out the fullness of the meaning of that love of which all human living is a progress of experience.

In Him is seen the articulation of what is experienced stage by stage in living from childhood to maturity. So obviously the whole basis of training will be to use the experience of love stage by stage, to reveal how that experience has been given eternal reality through Jesus Christ, and how, therefore, it will be through unity with Him that we shall be able ourselves to have the fullest mature understanding and experience in our own living of what love is. This is what the "new life in Christ" which is prayer means: it is the life which has cast out the insecurities, the fears, the things which make for death rather than life and which has understood what it means to live by a creative and life-giving love.

I do not wish to give any lengthy rules about the training in this understanding of life, as that would be to falsify the whole standpoint of my thinking which is that this kind of in-Christ living is not learned by rules. Rather will I indicate stage by stage what would be the factors of training which would correspond to the experience of love natural at that stage.

(1) *Infancy and early childhood*

Here the main experience is that of the need for emotional security, and such knowledge of love as the child has is confined to the narrow world of his mother, and, at a slightly later stage, of his father. His fear will be the loss of that love, his need will be the security of that love. The best training then that we can give at that age as mother and father is the experience of the kind of love which will help to give the child the confidence he needs and prepare him for the growth into maturity of his later life: such love will be neither the kind of smothering, possessive love which will wreak havoc with the maturity of later years, nor the lack of warm affection which may easily produce the anti-social delinquent. When the time comes for the articulation of this experience, we shall naturally help to give such concepts of God as to give the child the even greater sense of the security of the Love in which the love of his mother is grounded, the knowledge that what he knows is but the reflection of the security of the Reality behind it, that the arms of his mother express the arms of the everlasting God.

The stories of the life of Christ which express the security of the love which is never withdrawn are the infancy, the Parables of the Prodigal Son and of the Good Shepherd, the Christ with the children, even the Cross as the expression of the complete trust which love gives. The in-Christness at this stage which is likely to be most experienced is the experience of identification with the child Jesus, and His relationship with Our Lady. In fact, the symbolism of Mary the Mother is a very important symbolism which Protestants have repudiated and rejected to their impoverishment, because if Christian love is for most of us to be experienced through human love, the Fatherhood of God is not sufficient as an expression of experience. The child in his infancy and early years has much more relationship with mother than with father: the articulation of this needs an eternal Mother-figure, and this the Roman Catholics have been wise to recognize in the cult of Our Lady and which, perhaps, explains why Roman Catholicism has often seemed to be a religion of greater human warmth and understanding than the somewhat grim and austere front exhibited by so many brands of Protestantism.

(2) *Later childhood*

At this stage the child will begin to have experience of people outside the family circle: the close bonds with the mother should be loosened. The child will begin to realize his responsibilities towards other children; he will be conscious of the community life of the school; he may belong to other communities, and the need of a group to which he can belong and with which he may identify himself will be strong. Here then again the spirituality will be the articulation of experience.

We shall begin, both in the school religious instruction and in the home thinking, to let him see the real ty of Christ expressing itself through both the teaching of Chri t on responsibility towards others and his own living out of that responsibility. In the school, religious teaching will start from the child's own experience of both the difficulties and the tensions as well as the blessings and joys of community living; discussion will be encouraged about situations which arise in the school—the tensions in a classroom of the child who seeks undue attention and undermines community, the submerging of excessive individualism in group projects and games, the ability to face defeat in a game or failure in a subject, the jealousies of those who manage to come out first, whether in scholastic or athletic prowess. These are the kinds of things which will be part of the costliness of love in any community and will have to be worked through.

I well remember a very valuable lesson which started with discussion of the members of the class who sought attention, and those who came out ahead of the others in attainment; we faced the kind of difficulties which this causes, our own feelings about them, our own needs for attention, our own insecurities in our lesser attainment. The discussion was lively and the class were very much concerned with this as a living issue. We then set the class to discover whether there is any record of a similar situation in the life of any group with which Christ was concerned, and there naturally emerged the story of the claim of the mother of James and John for preference for her sons and the resentment this caused. We discussed Christ's way of dealing with this and we then considered how the in-Christ in us would deal with it today. The relevance of the living reality of Christ in coping with their own experiences of reality was very apparent.

In this period all training in spirituality will be concentrated on the spelling out of what in-Christ involvement in community means. This will take various forms apart from direct teaching. There will be experience of the difficulties and joys of sharing in the wider community of the Church, experience of Holy Communion and the laying of some understanding that Communion cannot be unless the price of community is being paid. There will be the beginning of understanding of the perspectives of the Lord's Prayer, the realization that forgiveness and reconciliation are within a wider context than that of relationship with mother and father. We are already beginning to help the child to understand the responsibilities of wider group relationships, and the parents are the bridge between themselves and the larger society outside the family.

At this point it will be particularly important what kind of standards in relation to the larger society the parents have made. The children will not be able to help forming their standards from what they hear and see in the home. Values on life will be beginning to be formed, which will either be working towards that unity of all living, which is the in-Christ relationship with all society, or working towards the egoistic destructiveness which will make a prayer relationship with the world impossible. If, therefore, the life of the parents is based upon an attitude of loving self-giving towards family, neighbourhood and work relationships, if there is the desire for service, the realization of mutual dependence, a lack of desire to dominate and to be self-sufficient—then the child will be living amidst the values which lead to that unity of living in which we can say "Our Father". If, on the other hand, the values of the parents are the desire to possess either riches or power, the desire to be independent of others, to do what they want to do, regardless of others—then the child will be inheriting the values of life in which a prayer relationship with God and others will become impossible because life will be centred not in constructive unity with the world around but in destructive opposition to society.

At this stage there will probably be much questioning, and it is likely that the questions will reveal an attempt to understand in quite down-to-earth terms what life is about. The teachers of prayer, whether parents or schoolteachers, will not only see their responsibility in dealing with such questions in a non-evasive and honest way, but will also be helping the child to vocalize his or her own experiences. A certain lay reader was once trying to explain to a group of children what paying attention to God in prayer meant, and he related the story of a lady in church who was exhibiting signs of restiveness during worship and at last got up and went out. Afterwards she explained to the lay reader that she had left something cooking and forgotten about it, and during the whole service she had been thinking of this and at last felt she must go home. The lay reader explained this as lack of attention to God. In discussion afterwards Mary, aged 12, said, "Perhaps God was telling her that if she didn't go home the meal would be spoilt and there might be a fire, which would be bad for her family and her home. Perhaps she was listening to God rather than to you conducting the service." That girl was already vocalizing an approach to prayer which understood its relevance to daily living in a way that the lay reader did not.

Let us, then, during this period learn from the way in which children speak of prayer and of life and of God, and the way in which they frame their reflections. Let the school assembly be worship largely made up of the vocalization of such experiences of living and understanding of community, and let there be the maximum participation of children expressing and acting out their understanding of an in-Christ relationship with life, however crude in form that expression may be.

(3) *Adolescence*

As we come to adolescence the experience from which we build our prayer takes another shift. The knowledge that we are coming to physical maturity brings the first known pressures of desire for sexual experience. Deeper than that, however, is the desire for emotional relationships which can become, although sometimes fleeting, very intense while they last. The desire for love turns away from the parents towards other young people of the same age group. There is the beginning of the seeking of a mate. Yet because there is such a great gap between physical and emotional maturity, between adulthood physically and adulthood sociologically and economically, this is also a time of great frustration which shows itself in "kicking against the pricks", resistance to authority, often real estrangement in outlook between parents and children. Rudeness and aggressiveness will often be the ways by which the first crude attempts to impose the recognition of adulthood upon society show themselves. There will be no belief too sacred to be questioned; the sacred cows of society will often be demolished quite ruthlessly; everything said by adults will be submitted to the most rigorous testing by experience, and dismissed if it does not make sense in experience. In the schools, Religious Instruction will be one of the subjects regarded as of "no use" because, like History, Music and

Geography, it does not seem to have much to help in the way of getting a job, which will be the main concern.

Yet side by side with all this, and indeed because of it, there will be a longing for what makes sense, for standards which work, for deep personal relationships, and for a cause which enables ideals to be expressed. Adolescence is often a time both of great loneliness and great enthusiasm: sometimes even the apparent cynicism masks a passionate desire to find a worth-while cause.

What then are the essentials of training in this period?

First, the opportunity given to express themselves freely and with complete openness, however "shocking" those ideas may sometimes seem to the adult world. This is a time when the kind of reflective meditation upon life and its meaning which I have expressed as the first part of prayer, the beginning of a "man in his wholeness wholly attending", may be made if the opportunities are given. The Religious Education master of a London comprehensive school asked the boys of his school to write a modern psalm based upon their own thinking of the way in which God did or did not fit into their lives, and what they were thinking about their lives. The results of these have been published in a remarkable book called *Modern Psalms by Boys* and reveal a great capacity for reflective thinking. Listen to this by an eleven-year-old boy:

> Through time men have worked together,
> They have built together and soon everything will be man-made.
> Did God mean this to happen?
> Does He know we are forgetting him—the Person who created us all?
> Why cannot we stop exactly where we are?
> Why do we have to go on?
> Is it the desire to build and construct?
> But the more things we desire the more we forget God.
> We are like animals stuffing ourselves with knowledge—but we must go on.

Is this not an almost exact description of what Bonhoeffer means when he says that man come of age will less and less use the God of the gaps?

Or take this cry of "Lord, I believe, help thou mine unbelief":

Who is God?
  What is God?
Is he really true?
  Does he work wonders?
I wish I knew.
Is he in the green trees?
  Is he in the meadow?
Is he in the latest beat?
  Is he in the twisting feet?
Is he real?
  Is he true?
I wish I knew.

Here in this writing and in that of a fifteen-year-old boy lies both the doubt and the wistfulness of the present day and age:

Under the hammer and sickle lie my views.
Be gone, wretched pulpit, priest and pew!
God is the state
And factory capacity; not heaven my bait.

but ending with:

Forward, let us march right on
To a Soviet Society with proud aplomb.
There will be factories, houses and
Offices to the sky, and—and—
In the end, just dust and sand.
Give me back my God.

I have quoted these (and there are many more that could be quoted) to show what can result from the opportunity given to reflect upon life and its meaning and the relevance or irrelevance of God. I have used in schools myself the *Prayers* of Michel Quoist, the *Litany of the Ghetto*, *Are you running with me, Jesus?* (Malcolm Boyd)—all of which seek to express from the experience of the situation and with contemporary language that kind of thinking about life which speaks to the needs of our time. Always when I have used these prayers they aroused an immediate response, save that sometimes boys have said that the scattering of the word "Lord" destroyed the real idea of God in the situation or the Spirit speaking through us rather than we talking to someone "out there". Let there then be the opportunity for the expression of life and its meaning with complete openness, and this will be the most relevant expression in word of an adolescent's understanding of prayer. I should hope that in the training of adolecents considerable use will be made of the schoolmaster's experiment mentioned above both in schools and in Confirmation classes, and that some of these modern books of prayers (of which I give a list under "Useful Books") will take the place of the usual Confirmation manual.

Secondly, it will be important that at this stage there is given such teaching on sexuality and group discussion of sexual and personal relationships that will get right away from the attitude to sexuality I have mentioned earlier in this book. This is the time at which the Church can emphasize the joy of sexual relationship, but side by side with this the responsibility of all deep relationships and their costliness. Group training will now include the beginning of training in group dynamics, or personal relationships in which, through the use of observers in small groups observing their behaviour, young people may begin to understand how they react upon each other, and how the group may be the means of bringing frustrations into the open and learning both acceptance of each other and release upon each other. It will be valuable to point out the way of using prayer as the release upon Christ of their hatreds and their loneliness in the way indicated when talking earlier about the purgative experience of such release. The group will also be the opportunity of learning, through bringing Biblical insights to bear upon case-studies of personal relationships (suggested case-studies for such use will be found in Appendix I to this book), what are the questions of responsibility which must be asked and faced in boy-girl friendship, and parent-child relationships.

Thirdly, the sphere of religious instruction in schools will properly be used to show what an in-Christ involvement in life means. This will be done by using the periods to relate the meaning which lies behind all other subjects taught in the school, to bring a unity of meaning into the various subjects of the syllabus, and so to inculcate an attitude to life which sees the lessons of history and science as building up a confidence and faith in the skill and progress of modern man and the need to work for the unity which those subjects reveal of nature and of man. In the same way, the study of biology, mathematics, psychology, and sociology, will be shown to reveal a rejoicing in the whole life of man, bodily, mentally, and spiritually. The study of geography and economics shows the inter-relationship of the needs of man and the concern which we must have for the satisfaction of those needs. In this way, the syllabus will not be just a collection of subjects but related to the whole understanding of the meaning of life: the illuminative and the unitive can come through the right approach in the Religious Instruction syllabus.

Fourthly, young people are ripe for the understanding of a modern asceticism. They are wanting a cause and are willing to bear the costliness of a cause. I remember seeing groups of young people, members of the Young Socialists, in Redhill one Saturday collecting for Famine Relief, and in order to bring point to the collection and realization of its meaning they had fasted for a whole week-end. I could have wished that there had been Youth Groups from the local Churches with them. This was a true understanding of what asceticism in modern life means. It is also evident in the considerable sacrifices which many young people make in Voluntary Service Overseas. I know of two young men from a comfortable home who manned a refugee camp in the hills of India and who underwent every hardship of semi-starvation, rough living and considerable personal danger. Young people need opportunities to fulfil their aspirations in enterprises that serve society rather than disrupting it, and to be able to cope with their innate aggressiveness in positive rather than negative ways. It should be our task to see that training in modern asceticism is providing for such opportunities.

Finally, I think it is important to remember that in the lives of many young people music plays an important part, and especially the beat music which is for many the background both to life and concentration. In spirituality training this must be used. A youth retreat, for example, might be an occasion when, instead of learning concentration in a background of silence which to many is distracting rather than helpful, there might be the background of that kind of "pop" music which often today contains a philosophy of reflection upon the meaning of life. One of the Beatles' recent records *Revolver* is an interesting illustration of this. The ballad of *Eleanor Rigby*[1] is about a lonely priest and a lonely spinster:

> Eleanor Rigby picks up the rice in a Church where a wedding has been,
> Lives in a dream
> Wearing the face that she keeps in a jar by the door,
> Who is it for?
> Father Mackenzie writing the words of a sermon that no-one will hear,
> No-one comes near
> Darning his socks at night when nobody's there.

with the haunting refrain:

> Look at all the lonely people, where do they all come from?

Or again the understanding of love's decay in the song, *For no one*: "She no longer needs you . . . a love that should have lasted years . . . in her eyes you see nothing." There is also a strange Tillichian sound in the last song: "Turn off your mind . . . lay down all thought: surrender to the voice: it is shining. That you may see the meaning of within: it is being". The background of songs such as these could well form the background to the reflective thinking of a youth retreat. Such could be followed by discussion in groups rather than by a conductor, when the themes could be further thought through as a basis for the next time of reflective thinking. Out of such groups might arise the vocalized prayer which sums up the thinking.

Adulthood

Training in adulthood would be the continuation of the training in adolescence with the remembrance that now we are coming to full maturity, in which the experience will be of many different types of relationship in work and neighbourhood, and with the added relationship of parenthood. Training in group relationships will now take into account such additional relationships, and group study will include the study of problems of work situations, the working out of what is the difference between the Christian and the non-Christian in the secular spheres of life, and what are the appropriate relationships to differing situations. The meaning of the in-Christ involvement in life which is the heart of prayer will have to include a much wider variety of situation than in adolescence, and it will probably be desirable that people involved in the same situation should meet to thresh out together what this involvement means in terms of their common problems. To this end we have at our Training Centre week-ends given over to managers, shop-stewards, teachers, clerks, architects, social workers and others, all trying to work through together the meaning of the experiences in which they find themselves in the secular world and the relevance of their prayer and worship to those situations.

The clergy will become more and more resource personnel in relation to these dialogues, more concerned with providing the means for such discussions to take place than seeing themselves as the leaders of such discussions. The function of the clergy will not be that of the old spiritual director who gave a rule of life and offered direction when problems were brought to him; rather will it be the function of the spiritual adviser to help a person to understand himself, to listen and go on listening, so that he may hear what lies behind the words in which problems are presented, and to help a man to discern for himself, or through mutual discussion and Bible Study with others, what is God's will and to respond to it. He may have to encourage a man to act when he sees what the action should be but lacks confidence to pursue it; he may have to give hope to a man in despair; he will enable people to see the consequences of various actions, to assess the responsibilities within the situation, to work through the prejudices and facades which are hiding the truth from themselves. But all these functions will be helping to set men free to be men come of age who can advance God's kingdom, hallow His name, seek acceptance, daily bread, and guidance for themselves and for others by the spirit of God working within them. It will not be the adviser's function to make people depend upon him but rather to help people to depend upon the Spirit and to understand what such dependence means.

Training will also include, through such group understanding and discussion, what are the pressures which a modern asceticism must resist—for the adult in modern society the pressures to want affluence and security will be strong, as will also be the pressures to social conformity. There will also be the pressures of overactivity, of a life in which there is never time for proper assessment and reflection. The learning of the costliness of the voluntary sacrifice of a standard of life which can be afforded in the interests of a greater need by others, the resistance of advertisement and social pressures, the deliberate making of time for a proper understanding of what we are doing and becoming—all these will form the kind of training in the asceticism which is appropriate to a mature man. The training will consist of the opportunity to look together at the pressures on our lives and to be able to assess objectively and honestly how far they are affecting us.

The other kind of costliness which must be learned is the costliness of parenthood. By this, I mean the realization of how and when to release our hold upon our children—that love is giving persons their true freedom, not possessing them for the satisfaction of ourselves. The best way of training for this is to provide means for confrontation between parents and young people so that each may speak openly and honestly to each other, and to provide support and help in guidance for parents when their children have left home and the mother especially may feel as if the purpose has gone out of life. The realization that not only the problems of youth but also the problems of middle-age have to be accepted and faced is not something that comes automatically but something over which guidance is needed from those who have experienced and successfully dealt with such problems.

Coburn, in his article from which I have already quoted, speaks of the problem of "prayer for busy people" by which he means the training which a man needs to make conscious to himself in the course of a day the in-Christ involvement with life which his personal reflection and group discussion have brought home to him. The title of Malcolm Boyd's book of prayers, *Are you running with me, Jesus?* brings this home. We need help to be not only involved but consciously involved with Christ: we have to have the reassurance that Christ is running with us in life and this is where the vocalization of our involvement becomes necessary: it is the spirit uttering within us. So it will be good to teach adults to use the moments of a busy day for such conscious affirmation of the presence of God as the recollection of responsibility for life while driving or the self-awareness which is able to say, "Get thee behind me, Satan", when tempted to drive aggressively or hoping to beat a pedestrian to a Belisha crossing. Again, why not use the time of strap-hanging in the underground for the kind of reflection which Quoist uses in his *Prayer in an Underground*, or for invoking the grace of God for the unknown standing next to one, unknown, but united in our common humanity before God. Can we not offer thanks in appreciation of life while walking, while having a pleasant meal, while listening to a concert, while having sexual intercourse, while enjoying close relationship with a friend—can there not be the conscious, "Thank you, God, for being in this with me," or "May the Christ within me be fulfilled in this enjoyment"? As Coburn says:

> The interior Dialogue of being mindful of God, thinking of him and responding in words from time to time as the expression of His spirit at work within throughout the day is as possible for a banker as for a farmer.

So all our training will be a means by which we can use experience to learn the prayer of reflective thinking, in-Christ involvement with life, asceticism which is relevant and the supportive group, the "religious community". At each stage we shall use that stage of experience which is most appropriate: we shall proceed step by step in line with the principle "I sat where they sat" and as soon as possible we shall use the group so that we may learn from each other; at each stage our task will be to start from the experience and in the light of that experience to understand both the nature of the involvement to which we are called and the eternal dimension of meaning which is to be expressed in that involvement. That is why the method will usually be the group method and will entail the linking together of biblical study and contemporary case-situations.

I think the methods I have outlined will do much to help people to practise the four-fold method of modern prayer which it has been the task of this book to develop—the pattern of a life of reflection, involvement, asceticism and community, and so to find a prayer which speaks to their condition and to their needs.

CHAPTER 9

CORPORATE PRAYER: A RELEVANT WORSHIP

The aim of this book has been mainly to work out a relevant personal spirituality by which a man may live his daily life, rather than to be concerned with the action of the gathered people of God in the activity we usually call public worship. I cannot, however, conclude without devoting the last chapter to this activity because the two are closely interlinked and because public worship is, or should be, the corporate expression week by week of all that is being expressed in personal spirituality during the week. When a Christian worships he is not doing something contrary to his private prayer. He is expressing in a community action the corporate nature of all spirituality. He is expressing the fact that the people of God are not a collection of individuals all finding their own separate ways to communication with God and with men, but that the people of God are also a *gathered* people who need, as the first apostles needed, to "meet together week by week to share the common life, to break bread and to pray". Christ took flesh to become the head of a body, the new people of God, and at worship we have an encounter in faith with Christ and with each other. Such an encounter will need things which we can have in common—signs, symbols, actions and words. There will need to be common forms by which we can show publicly what we mean by an in-Christ relation to life; in life, communication occurs through the use of the material and the physical, so we shall need common expressions of this in sign and symbol: in life, communication occurs through language, so we shall need a common language. The important fact is that worship shall really express what we are trying to *say* about the meaning of life and what we are trying to *be* as the people of God.

This is where we seem to fall down. The boy who said to me that for him the Church spells boredom is saying what so many feel—boredom or irrelevance. The majority of people do not see any connection between what they call "going to church" and the activities and difficulties of everyday life. They do not see any visible connection between the reciting of psalms of two thousand years ago, the singing of hymns which convey a picture of a God either terribly remote or only desirous that one should grovel before Him in abject subjection, the preaching of sermons which are mainly moralistic, and life as they know it. Nor is this sense of irrelevance only found in those outside the Church worship. Those who do worship so often give the impression that their attitude to worship is simply a matter of individual preference. "I go to the kind of service I like" is the usual reaction, and if the service becomes the kind of service I don't like, then I stay away—it is as simple as that. But where does any concept of worship lie in that attitude? Where is there any expression of the gathered people of God?

Our common worship, if it is to be along the lines which have been worked out in this book, must be so shaped that it expresses and communicates the meaning of life, involvement with life, the costliness of that involvement, and our need for community. There will be two groups whose needs we shall constantly be bearing in mind as we frame our worship. First, there will be the group of those who are already within the membership and ministry of the Church, who have committed themselves in that they wish to belong, have in varying degrees made an act of faith in the reality of God and wish to be involved with Him in service within His world. For them the problem will be how to express that sense of belonging and that relationship of service to the needs of men in daily living within a corporate framework of word and action which is meaningful of this to them and reasonably simple of comprehension to others. But there will be another group who are most important in considering forms of worship: the quite large group of people who feel that as yet they cannot commit themselves, but who are more with us than against us in that they are concerned with the great questions of living, who are desirous of being in dialogue and even in some kind of community with those who are members, and who are willing to share in some kind of common expression in word and action of what they feel about life, provided means of expression may be discovered which speak to their needs. The Bishop of Woolwich describes these two groups as those who are Members, and those who are Meeting, that is, willing to meet us but not yet in full membership. There will then be a need to work out what one might call common experiences of reflection upon life where Members and "Meeters" may join in that sense of the meaning of the word "worship" which is "expressing worth", the worth of what we are thinking, the worth of what we are meaning. We shall then be concerned with two kinds of corporate spirituality—the first being, how can the liturgy of the Church really say what we mean about life and involvement in and through Christ; the second, how can we devise forms which will express the need for encounter between those who are members and those who are meeting in a dialogue of reflective thinking or dramatic action, which will speak to the needs and understanding of both?

The Eucharist as the Expression of Membership Worship

The contemporary liturgical movement is rightly concerned with the Eucharist because the Eucharist is pre-eminently the expression of the in-Christ relationship with the world:

> The Eucharist is *the* Christian action, the heart of all Christian action in the world, because it mediates and makes present in all its efficacy and power the great saving act of God in Christ once and for all wrought out on Calvary. For all Christian action in this world is really nothing else than the finished work of Christ becoming operative through His body the Church. This is the point when all Christian action begins, where we are united with His act where what He has done for us is renewed within us for transmission to the world. (Bishop of Woolwich, *Liturgy Coming to Life*)

If we are members of His body, of His flesh, of His bones, we are Christ: "I live; yet not I, but Christ liveth in me." (Gal. 2: 20) This is what we are trying to express in the Eucharist. It is the corporate showing forth of what in-Christ involvement with life means, and is a showing forth of a *common* action. This is the significance of liturgical prayer which is the beginning and the ending of all private prayer—here we are all bound into one bundle, we are offered by Christ in His body to the Father and our life is renewed by Him. This is "being in Christ", and nowhere is expressed more completely than in the Eucharist the unity of all life: love in Christ, Christ's love in us, our love for our neighbour because he is ourself. What we are being called to today is a new understanding of unity in Christ—unity with God, unity with each other; unity with ourselves, because we are members of His flesh and of His bones.

All the four-fold aspects of contemporary spirituality which I have quoted are worked through in the Eucharist and its actions. First, it is an act of recalling and of reflection: it is the recalling and re-enacting of the mighty acts of God in creation, redemption and resurrection—the whole meaning of life is expressed in this outward and visible sign that nothing in life is secular but all has been made sacred in its origin by God, that we are to look for God in the midst and not at the boundaries of life as Christ was discovered at Emmaus in the breaking of the bread. It is also the meaning of life in relation to ourselves, that being in Christ is our true nature, what we are meant to be, the self-affirmation of our real nature in its truest sense. As St Augustine said to his communicants, "If then you are the body of Christ and his members then that which is on the altar is the mystery of ourselves. Receive the mystery of yourselves."

Secondly, it is an act of involvement both of ourselves with Christ and of ourselves with each other; it is an offering of God's creative world by man to God and the receiving back of the presence of Christ in that creative world with the intention that we shall then carry into the world not just ourselves but Christ in ourselves. We and all our life, our work, our politics, our home, and our personal relationships, are taken, offered in all their poverty as well as their goodness at the altar in the confidence that, however imperfect, they are accepted. The offertory is symbolic recognition that daily work and daily life are not just things with no meaning or purpose beyond the getting of money by which to live but the presenting of what we are to the creator of what we are. But, as I have said, it is an involvement with Christ that is taken back into the world; worship is lived. It is the life of Christ in the life of Christians. To be His body in the world we need to partake of His body in the corporate liturgy of the Church.

Thirdly, it is an action which expresses the meaning of Christian asceticism: "he took" but also "he broke". It is in the identification with the broken body that we realize all that has to be mortified and broken in us if we are to be His body to the world. We are called to realize in every Eucharist that the breaking is an integral part of the triumph of the life of love, for love is costly. The world is to be redeemed, not accommodated—a task the Church has often been slow to recognize. The recognition of the pressures which are upon us just to be accommodating is the recognition that we who partake of the Eucharist cannot expect just lives of ease without pain or disturbance. As Bouyer puts it so well in his book, *Life and Liturgy*:

> Mystery is not to comply with the ways of the world but to take hold of the world, to struggle with it even to death, and only to master it finally in the Resurrection.

The liturgy must be so expressed in the words used and in the actions which follow or in which it is set that

> . . . the test of worship is how far it makes us more sensitive to the beyond in our midst, to the Christ in the hungry, the naked, the homeless and the prisoner. (Bishop of Woolwich, *Honest to God*)

Finally, the Eucharist is the expression of community, for it is the joint action of the people of God, not something the clergy do for the laity, but something in which all have a part, in which the limbs of the Body of Christ are seen acting as a community. We come to the liturgy not only to receive the Body of Christ but to *be* the Body of Christ. This means that the liturgical action must be seen to be the action of the whole Church, clergy and laity, in which each has a part to play. It means also that Communion will only be obvious if it arises out of existing community and is the expression of a group life in which the acceptance and tensions of community life have been experienced. Just as the liturgical action is the pattern of all Christian action in the world, so the liturgical society is the pattern of all society redeemed by Christ.

Making Real the Liturgy

How then shall the reality of all this be actually expressed in the liturgy? I shall content myself with saying what *must* be in the composition and use of any liturgy if it is to feed the faith of those within the Church and show its meaning to those outside.

(a) *The words and actions of the liturgy*

There should be two main considerations in the words and actions of the Eucharist: that they should express the meaning of what is being said and done in terms which are familiar to the ears and eyes of this century, and they should be in simple but good language which conveys neither a sense of the archaic nor an ephemeral colloquialism from which all sense of timelessness has departed. It is these facts which should determine the structure of liturgy and not a constant looking to past liturgies or even to an obsession with a literary beauty of language couched in words which take us also to the past rather than the present. It always seems to me that one of the difficulties of liturgical revision in the Church of England is that each revision seems to start from the liturgy of a previous Prayer Book rather than starting with what liturgy is meant to express and how best in this age it can be expressed. I would like to see the scholars of the Liturgical Commission asking themselves very simply the question: what meaning do we want this liturgy to convey and how may we order and word it that this meaning is most clearly communicable both to those who are taking part and to those who are seeking to know its meaning?

This means that we shall want to see a Confession which speaks simply to the needs of men to find acceptance, and to our sin in hiding our true selves from God and from each other; it will be a simple acknowledgement of sin in words which are neither emotionally loaded or grovelling, brief, to the point, and making clear from the wording what we mean by sin.

The Proclamation of the Word for the Day should be clear in what it is proclaiming by the ordering of Collect, Old Testament Lesson, Epistle and Gospel, so that a particular Christian theme or proclamation of God's truth is running through it, clearly observable to the worshipper and to the preacher, whose task will be to relate that theme to the situation of the congregation in their wrestling with that Word in the secular world.

The Offertory needs not only action but some form of words indicating that this is the offering of man's creative life to the author of creation, and the assurance that this offering is accepted. I find it very difficult to understand the objections now being made in Evangelical theological circles to the explicit statement of this offering. It seems to be based on the idea that man can have nothing to offer, which not only seems to be theologically false in the doctrine of creation and the true nature of man and his dignity, but also to be attempting to deprive the liturgy of what is very real in the connection between life and in-Christ involvement with life.

In the Eucharistic Prayer itself there should not be the heavy concentration on the Passion of Christ to the exclusion of the Resurrection and the Ascension or of his final glory in the mystical Body. The Eucharistic Prayer should be a prayer of the new life in Christ, the great Reality underlying all earthly realities, a thanksgiving to God for all His gifts, bringing home to everyone who partakes the meaning of life as life in its fullness and strength to be enjoyed in Christ: creation, preservation, redemption and resurrection—the notes of joy and power. These are the words which can both make sense and give hope to a world which has rather lost its sense of the joy and power of life. There has been a decided improvement in this respect in the new Liturgy suggested for three years experimental use and, at the moment of writing, passed unanimously by all Houses of Convocation; but even in the new Liturgy there is not sufficient emphasis upon the new life. The experimental liturgy used at St Mary's Abbey, West Malling, although rather verbose for modern use, brings this out most of any that I have seen: "We offer unto thee thine own of thine own, from all and for all, the holy bread of eternal life and the cup of everlasting salvation . . . that all who partake . . . be gathered into one and filled with thy grace and heavenly benediction . . . thou dost make us a holy people worthy to stand and minister before thee." Again, the response of the people in the St Mark's liturgy (*see* Appendix 2) brings home this sense of new life in Christ by which and in which we approach the world: "Come, risen Lord. Live in us that we may live in you." It is this kind of emphasis in liturgy which formalizes into our worship something of the great vision of the living unity of all things in God which we owe to Teilhard de Chardin.

After the receiving of Communion there is need for little else save an expression of thanks (even this may not be necessary, the receiving is its own thanks) and a dismissal which indicates clearly that the action of the Eucharist is now to become involvement with the world, and we are to offer ourselves, freed and given new life by Him, to be His Body in the world: "Go. You are free. Serve the Lord and His people."

All this must be expressed in the simplest of good English. Here is still the difficulty. Excellent as the Revised service is, it is still couched in a language which is stylized and abounds in "thee" and "thou". As the Bishop of Woolwich says of the new service:

> It leaves the language basically untouched. It may get us out of the seventeenth century but it does not get us into the twentieth. It suspends us, in fact, in an artificial liturgical world of its own unrelated to space or time, in which nobody really lives. (Article in *New Christian*, July 14, 1966)

Is it so impossible to find the persons who can write good English in the style and with the terms of this century? Recently there have been several books of prayers and meditations written which do this very thing (*Creative Brooding* by Robert Raines; *That man is you* by Louis Evely; *Spilled Milk* by Kay Smallzried). Let someone now work on the new Liturgy with new language, which will enable not only the thought but also the words to live. I am not suggesting that we want second-rate verbosity such as some modern prayers give us but rather the best examples of modern English, in the same way that we would expect a modern Church or a modern painting to reflect the best architecture and art of the twentieth century and not of the sixteenth.

The actions of the Eucharist also must be such as to suggest by visual aid the meaning of what we are doing and its relevance to and involvement in our lives. The following will, therefore, be important in the way of "doing" the Eucharist:

(i.) The altar set in the midst and the priest facing the people is itself a symbol of the Christ in the midst of life and of the "open-ness" of priest and people to each other—the openness of action signifying the openness of the Christian community.

(ii.) The Constitution on the liturgy in the Vatican Council speaks of the value of the concelebration of the clergy as signifying the *unity* of the whole celebrating community in the act which itself speaks of the unity of God with His world. Dom Placid Murray, O.S.B., commenting on this in an article in *The Way* says:

> Here then is a case where the clarifying of the sign has linked up eucharist and life, sacrament and community. It has made the rite an "open" one, opening out immediately into life, not a closed one, carried out as something rounded off in itself. (*The Way*, October 1966)

(iii.) The use of an ordinary loaf on a bread-board and an ordinary bottle of wine such as would normally be drunk, rather than a special ecclesiastical wafer or wine, brings home forcibly that the offering presented is an offering of the ordinary life as imperfect as ordinary bread is imperfect and yet as related to life as food and drink are related to life.

(iv.) In the same way the presentation of the offering by the laity either in family, occupational, or neighbourhood groups, symbolizes the various spheres of life which are offered to Christ and needing to be filled with His presence.

(v.) If we are to present the Eucharist as the act of the whole people of God it must involve the maximum of clergy-lay participation. Not only may many of the prayers be said together by celebrant and congregation, but also the Epistle and Gospel may normally be read by a layman or lay woman, the bidding prayers before the Prayer for the Church, or its equivalent in terms of a litany of response, can be spoken out by members of the congregation so that the involvement needs of each may become the involvement needs of all. The sermon itself could sometimes be delivered by members of the laity and could be the expression before the whole congregation of the group thinking going on in the parish during the week. This has often been done with groups meeting at our Training Centre when sermon, intercessions, choice of hymns, have all been the result of the group thinking and the expression of group need placed before the whole Conference in its Eucharistic worship on the Sunday. The receiving of Communion standing with each member first giving the greeting of the Kiss of Peace or its equivalent to each other, and then passing bread and cup to each other emphasizes the inter-relationship between communion with each other and communion with Christ. Perhaps also the dismissal for service back in the world could appropriately be given by a layman, as in former days the "Ite Missa Est" was given by the deacon.

(b) *The need for much local experiment before formalization of liturgy*

In an age of mobility it could be suggested that there should be a standardized form of worship so that wherever people went they would have the security of finding worship expressed in much the same way. But there is another argument. A mobile society will be a society which takes more easily to change and which will more readily see the point of letting worship arise out of the needs of the local situation so that the experience forms the background of the expression of that experience in worship. It may well be that we need both. We need to be working on a liturgy which as far as is possible with any liturgy can be reasonably timeless and recognizable as the same in all circumstances for the general worship of the Church. Equally we need much greater freedom to work out local liturgies which shall meet the needs and experience of a local situation. For example, the house communion, or the communion arising from an ecumenical or occupational group, or again the communion which is to precede a group engaged in a common act of service, or a Parochial Church Council, a parish social or dance, may need a much simpler form, with more down-to-earth language and greater spontaneity of both confession and intercession than would be either desirable or appropriate for a universal liturgy. Such a liturgy will not be intended for all times and all places and will not need votes by Convocation, only the permission of the Bishop to recognize when the situation demands a free experimentation when the groups themselves may not only draw up and discuss their forms but also try them out and discard what does not ring true in their experience. It may well be that, although such liturgies are only intended for particular use, valuable material will come from them which may well find its place in future liturgies for general use. Of such a kind is the Liturgy prepared at St Mark's, New York, for use on special ecumenical occasions and in a college situation, given in Appendix 2 to this book, and which has been found invaluable with certain local corrections for use in similar situations and with similar groups at the Southwark Training Centre.

(c) *Communion arising from experienced community*

The above brings me to my last point about the Eucharist itself in contemporary worship. Whatever alterations we make to the words or actions of the Eucharist it will make little impact of relevance on an empirical world unless it is seen to arise out of real community. The disciples met together in Communion because they were in everyday life a fellowship, a *koinonia* of love, finding their focus in Christ. Is it possible for a large congregation to be a community and is it possible, therefore, for there to be real communion? Father Godfrey Diekmann, O.S.B., writes in *Worship* (November 1965):

> Another hindrance to the Eucharist affecting a true people of God is the obstacle of a congregation so large that even the Eucharist cannot make of it a community . . . already Plato recognized that community ceases where personal relationships become impossible. The structuring of the people of God into mammoth congregations instead of communities would seem to be the greatest long-range pastoral and therefore liturgical problem facing the American Church.

It might seem ironic with the state of many of our tiny congregations to talk of this as an obstacle, but it is still true in many a suburban church with over a hundred communicants each Sunday. Is not the vast Earl's Court evangelism of the Billy Graham pattern a barrier to true community? Is not, equally, the vast crowd at a Roman Mass? Should we not welcome rather than deplore that we are once again working with small groups which can learn together the group relationships out of which Holy Communion may once again be an expression of a holy community knowing, loving and caring for each other in that released accepting love which has cast out fear. Will not Holy Communion really be a therapeutic experience in such a group, speaking in a way that it does not speak in a crowded church where the next-door neighbour at the altar rail is not even known by name? What I am saying, or rather thinking aloud, is that, perhaps, we should reverse the idea which has been growing of the great Parish Communion, the gathering of the whole people of God into the one service of worship and let Communion be de-centralized, but not into many Masses in church on Sundays, but into many Communions arising out of groups experiencing and knowing community together on week-days, so that when they do come together it will be a togetherness of many communities which have found Communion, rather than a togetherness of a large group which cannot find Communion as a large group. Then the Parish Communion would at least arise out of experienced community within the many groups gathered there, and the groups might then go on from there to forge their links with the other groups on a different relationship basis in the larger whole. The possibility of the great extension of the priest-worker movement would make this possible because there might then well be in many small groups those commissioned to perform the priestly function.

In the same way, is not the true test of a valid Communion rather the experience of real community than the question of Orders and Forms? Have we not put the cart before the horse?

I would say that when Anglicans, Roman Catholics and Free Churchmen have been working together on some act of service or some study and prayer and have found real community of love between each other and in-Christ togetherness, then Communion is not only fitting but should result from such experienced community. This should be the test of a valid inter-Communion. If there has not been this working together, then occasional services of inter-Communion will do more harm than good, for they will be truly invalid, arising from no genuine understanding of each other in loving community.

Other Suggestions for a Corporate Membership Spirituality

If we are to take the full participation of the laity and clergy as the whole people of God seriously, this will also mean a much greater degree of co-operation in the planning of the membership worship of the Church. For too long has it been assumed that the planning of the thinking and worshipping life of the Church is the task of the clergy. Is there not a proper place in the parish for a local liturgical commission of the clergy and laity, working out together the pattern of preaching—what the people of God need to hear of the Word of God in the coming months, and what are the lay problems to which that preaching must be geared—the method and content of the Lent Course, the manner and form of the worship on other occasions than the Eucharist? I know of one parish where the clergy and laity work out together each year the Lent Course, and as a result there is maximum support because it has not been imposed upon the laity by the clergy but has been the result of their joint thinking and planning.

The method of conducting Retreats also needs looking at. Why is it always assumed that Retreats for laity must be conducted by clergy and usually that retreats for clergy must be conducted by Religious? Have the clergy a special prerogative in guiding the laity in an understanding of "holy worldliness", and have Religious necessarily an insight into the problems of parish clergy? Is it not possible that a retreat for laymen and women would be often better conducted by another layman who has given real thought to the insights of the faith into the secular world? I would also suggest the possibility of further developments in the method of the Retreat where, instead of a conductor, the thoughts for the times of silence should arise from the group thinking after periods of discussion on a theme. This has been used at Wychcroft with young people (see p. 82) and with ordinands, and has been found a greater incentive to interior reflection on the meaning of daily life than talks by conductors. John Coburn emphasizes this point in his article in *Worship*:

> Where is the place of the "holy community"? Indeed is it not the "holy people of God" rather than the "holy man of God" of which the Bible most often speaks? This means some measure of guidance through small groups where intimate sharing and listening is possible. (*Worship*, Vol. 39, No. 10, p. 624)

The Worship of Meeting

Besides the worship of the Eucharist, there will be need for corporate expression of a worship which can meet the needs of both members and those who cannot yet see their way to the commitment of membership but are aware of their common searchings for an understanding of life. Worship is not going off into a world which we call the religious world. Worship is the understanding of the worth of things; it is the understanding of the worth of ourselves, the worth of the world, the lack of worth when there is not true understanding and appreciation of life, the lack of worth in ourselves when we live at a lower level than our true nature. Worship is not intended to make us religious. It is intended to make us human. For to be human is to be made in the image of God. To be human is to be measured by the full stature of humanity in Christ.

Now you may wonder why at this point I am saying all this. I am saying this because there are many people who may not yet have recognized explicitly the sense of the God who has "got the whole world in His hands", or consciously measured their own maturity by the fullness of the stature of Christ, but who are equally concerned with us about the world, who are passionately longing for an understanding of what true human maturity is, and have a desire to find their own true worth. These are our common concerns as men. These then should be expressed in the common worship which we have between

Christians and those ready to meet Christians. All forms of worship outside the Eucharist should be a liturgy-making by communities expressive of their common search for the worth of man, their common concern for the needs of man, their common recognition of the insecurities of man.

I do not think the kind of worship which is designed for the meeting of Christians and those who are turned towards us but not yet fully with us should be in fixed forms at all. Neither Matins nor Evensong meets the needs of this situation, and they are in any case so bound up with the Jewish background to our faith that to many they seem just an imposition of tedium rather than the natural expression of the community. As a fixed form the Roman Catholic service of Benediction is better because it is a simple act of adoration easily understood, and at least expresses the need of appreciation, the measuring of ourselves by the stature of Christ, and an obvious connection with the Eucharist, but the localization of Christ within the Church which it implies destroys the values of its simplicity. We do not need fixed forms, however. We do need the community which is gathered together to work out the forms which are an attempt to put into words the community's understanding of itself and its needs, its own evaluation of its worth or lack of worth. This will mean the use of modern language, material from modern plays and novels, hymns and music, which in word and tune speak to the needs of the community at worship. The form of the worship, whether in spoken word, actions, use of drama, must be entirely free to the purposes of those who are trying to express through it their humanity.

There have recently been some exciting attempts to do this, especially by young people, of which examples are: a Leavers Service at Greenwich, in which the desire for freedom and the pressures which in the modern world inhibit freedom were the theme of the service; a service arranged by a Youth Group at St Andrew's, Edgware, entitled "Be Yourself", which speaks its own message of self-understanding and evaluation; and at Clifton College some very interesting services involving full use of modern novels and drama on themes such as "Uncertainty",

"Change", "Life after Death", have lifted School Worship from a deadly boredom into a living reality. I have printed three examples of this kind of service in Appendix 3 to this book.

I have already illustrated the kind of prayer which speaks to the involvement of modern man by the use of quotations from books of prayers such as those of Michel Quoist, Malcolm Boyd, *Modern Psalms by Boys* (this to me is one of the most thrilling collections of all for its simple honesty and considerable beauty), Father Louis Evely, the *Litany of the Ghetto*, and such a prayer as William Opel's *Seeing and Praying* (see *New Christian*, Sept. 8, 1966). Many of these are only possible for private use, but some are suitable with slight adaptation for community worship and there is need for considerable extension of this form of prayer for public use and above all for hymns which can be sung without embarrassment and with meaning in this present age. What we need is not only the discovery of the words which speak to the mind and imagery of the modern world but also music which is good and contemporary and congregational, both for the Eucharist and the Worship of Meeting.

"Worship," as Eric James points out in a very good speech on this subject to American Methodists, "will always be thrusting us from God's world of the gathered Church into that world of His which waits for His kingdom and in which His kingdom is coming." It is because Michel Quoist's prayers look to God in ordinary situations and needs in the world, and find God already present there, calling men to their full maturity, that they have captured the imagination of many who feel in them an authentic spirituality for their time. It is this authentic spirituality which should also grow from the common life and worship of the Body of Christ, expressing itself in the ways and forms of worship both of the Eucharist and of free forms. One of the boys in *Modern Psalms by Boys* contrasts primitive worship with modern and asks:

> The Water they worshipped, for it was their drink,
> The earth they worshipped, for it was their home.
> They had cause to worship these "gods",
> But what cause is there to worship You?

It is because we have not presented our worship so that God is seen to be the food, the drink, the home, the life which is our own essential humanity, that worship is deemed irrelevant and boring. Let it be the task of this age not only to find a praying of life personally but also a praying of life corporately.

Conclusion

So I come to the end of this book. There is much that has been left out, much more that could be said. My hope is that the kind of way to a relevant prayer for today which I have indicated may be developed more thoroughly by others who are better qualified than I to do this. I realize that all the way through this book there seems to have been little separation between the living of life and prayer. If you have felt this you have really understood what I have been trying to say. I do not believe there is a proper separation between life and prayer. I believe that all life is response to God and that it is in life that we make our response. If we from time to time withdraw, it is only that we may have time to reflect on what our response should be. To affirm God in every circumstance of life, and to affirm God because God is the reality behind all life; "all things affirm thee in living" (T. S. Eliot: *Murder in the Cathedral*): that to me is prayer, and I have tried to spell out in different ways how that affirmation is made, and how we may be trained or helped to make it.

Earlier in this book I mentioned that a man at our Training Centre once asked: "Teach me to pray my life." If anything I have written in this book helps him and others to do that very thing, that is the only reason and sufficient reason for the writing of this book.

APPENDIX I

CASE-STUDIES
FOR USE IN TRAINING YOUNG PEOPLE

(*see page* 94)

1. John and Joan are "steady" boy and girl friends. They have known each other for some while. One night at a party John attempts to have sexual relationships with Joan which she resists. This causes a quarrel between them and John says, "Other girls let their boy friends do this with them. If you really loved me you would do the same because you know I would take all precautions." Joan does not want to lose her virginity but she doesn't want to lose John, and she is afraid that she will do so if she does not let him have his way. Her other friends tell her she should and say, "You'll never keep any boy if you don't give him all he wants." What is Joan to do, and how is she to convince John of her point of view and yet keep his love?

2. Derek and Phyllis are firm friends but Phyllis is very possessive and wants Derek to spend most evenings with her. Derek is anxious to pass exams and knows that this will mean some evenings must be spent in work; also, he likes to have some evenings with his mates. Phyllis feels hurt every time she rings him up and he cannot see her. He wants to keep her friendship but does not want to be tied to such a deep relationship. After a while he suspects that Phyllis is already thinking in terms of marriage, but he has no wish to get married until he is much more surely settled in his work. How are they to sort out these difficulties in viewpoint without breaking up the relationship, which neither desires?

3. Joan is irritated by the fact that every time she goes out for the

evening her mother wants to know where she is going and what time she will be in. Joan is eighteen. Her mother is worried because she always arrives home late at night and she feels she has the right to know where her daughter is. Also, when Joan is at home she likes to have the record-player on very loud with "pop-music" which her father hates: he likes everyone to be quiet so that he can watch television. This Joan finds deadly dull so she goes out even more. At last she announces that she is going to leave home and share a flat with another girl friend. How is this division between the generations to be reconciled? Will it be a good thing that Joan should leave home?

4. Michael goes to Grammar School and has made friends with a group of boys whose parents are much better off than his. He is continually demanding things and money which will enable him to keep up with these friends and resents his parents not being able to supply these needs. One night there is a full-scale row between him and his father over the latest demand for a motor-bike. How is his father to convince him? How can he keep his friends without worrying about "keeping up with the Jones"?

APPENDIX 2

A EUCHARISTIC LITURGY

Prepared at St. Mark's, New York, for use on special ecumenical occasions. (With some amendments).

THE PREPARATIONS

(Priest and people standing.)

Celebrant: We are here

People: IN THE NAME OF JESUS CHRIST.

Celebrant & people: WE ARE HERE BECAUSE WE ARE MEN—BUT WE DENY OUR HUMANITY. WE DO NOT LOVE OTHERS. WE HIDE FROM EACH OTHER AND FROM OUR TRUE SELVES. WE WAR AGAINST LIFE. WE HURT EACH OTHER. WE ARE SORRY FOR IT AND WE ARE SICK FROM IT. WE SEEK NEW LIFE.

Celebrant: Giver of life, heal us and free us to be men.

Celebrant & people: HOLY SPIRIT SPEAK TO US. HELP US TO LISTEN FOR WE ARE VERY DEAF. COME, FILL THIS MOMENT.

(Silence for a while. Sitting or kneeling.)

THE SERVICE OF THE WORD

The Collect.

The Old Testament Lesson.

The Epistle.

Hymn.

The Gospel.

Sermon (*if to be given*).

Intercessions. (*The celebrant shall lead the biddings, and then call for biddings from the people, with or without a litany and response.*)

THE OFFERTORY

Celebrant: If you are offering your gift at the altar, and there remember that your brother has something against you, leave your gift at the altar and go, first be reconciled to your brother and then come and offer your gift.
(*After which he will turn to the people and say:*)
Peace my friends.

People: AND PEACE TO YOU.

(*Then the priest shall read words from Romans* 12: 1–2; *after which the offerings will be made while a hymn is sung.*)

THE ACT OF THANKSGIVING

Celebrant: The Lord be with you.

People: AND WITH YOU.

Celebrant: Lift up your hearts.

People: WE LIFT THEM TO THE LORD.

Celebrant: Let us give thanks for God's glory.

People: WE GIVE THANKS. WE REJOICE IN LIFE. IN THE GLORY OF ALL CREATION.

Celebrant: All glory to you O Father who sent your only son into the world to be a man born of a woman's womb to die for us on a cross that was made by us.

People: HE CAME FOR US. HELP US TO ACCEPT HIS COMING.

Celebrant: He walked among us, a man upon earth, in our world of conflict and commanded us to remember His death, His death through which came new life: and to wait for His coming into glory in our lives.

People: WE REMEMBER HIS DEATH. WE LIVE BY HIS PRESENCE. WE WAIT FOR HIS COMING.

Celebrant: *(He takes the bread).* On the night He was betrayed the Lord Jesus took bread, He gave thanks; He broke it and gave to His disciples saying: "Take eat, this is my body. Do this for the recalling of me." *(He takes the wine).* He also took the cup: He gave thanks and gave it to them, saying: "Drink of it all of you. This is my blood which is poured out for many for the forgiveness of sins."

People: COME, LORD JESUS, COME.

Celebrant: Therefore remembering His death, believing in His rising, longing to recognise His presence: now in this place we obey His command: We offer bread and wine, we offer ourselves to be used.

People: EVERYTHING IS YOURS, O LORD. WE RETURN THE GIFT WHICH FIRST YOU GAVE US.

Celebrant: Accept it O Father. Send down the spirit of life and power glory and love upon us all, upon this bread and wine, that to us they may be His body and blood.

People: COME RISEN LORD. LIVE IN US THAT WE MAY LIVE IN YOU.

Celebrant: Now with all men who ever were, are and will be, with all creation and in all time with joy we sing:

All: HOLY HOLY HOLY LORD GOD ALMIGHTY. ALL SPACE AND ALL TIME SHOW FORTH YOUR GLORY NOW AND ALWAYS. AMEN.

Celebrant: And now in His words we are bold to say:

All: OUR FATHER . . . AMEN.

Then shall the celebrant break bread before the people saying:

Celebrant: The gifts of God for the people of God.

All: AMEN.

THE COMMUNION

Then shall the celebrant receive communion and distribute to all present with the words:

Celebrant: The body of Christ.

Communicant: AMEN.

Celebrant: The blood of Christ.

Communicant: AMEN.

(*When all have communicated, the remaining elements shall be consumed while a hymn is sung.*)

THE DISMISSAL

Celebrant: Go. You are free. Serve the Lord and His people.

People: AMEN.

APPENDIX 3

AN EXPERIMENT IN WORSHIP AT CLIFTON COLLEGE FEBRUARY 14, 1965

UNCERTAINTY

"Man is made for the vision of God—that is all he *is* made for." Or is he? There is a lot of disagreement when the question "What is man made for?" is debated. The view that we are made by God and for God is not a view about which there can be said to be general agreement, neither in the world at large nor in the chapel here this evening.

Whether we believe in God or not, we still have to work out for ourselves an answer to the question "Who or what am I?" And that question also, like the question "Is man made for God?" is a question to which most people have difficulty in having an absolutely certain answer.

The subject of this evening's service is "Uncertainty". The service is in three parts.

Part One

Uncertainty about the role and nature of Christianity

Five passages by contemporary writers will be read which represent, between them, a broad range of opinion about the nature and role of Christianity. Each is expressed in vivid terms, and there can be no-one here who will agree with all five. Everyone is likely to disagree with the viewpoint, and perhaps also with the tone, of at least one of the passages. The questions which are raised include the following:

"How can you be moral, and what help can Christianity give?"

"Does Christianity do more harm than good?"

"If you do give up Christianity, do you then 'carry Hell around inside you'?"

"If you do give up the old morality, what do you put in its place?"

"But *why* give up Christianity, *why* give up the old morality? —'Man is made for the vision of God. That is all he *is* made for.' "

Several shorter passages will be read to remind us that there is a similar diversity of opinion, and a similar uncertainty, amongst members of this evening's congregation. Further, there are a number of people here who are opposed to this service, this kind of service, taking place—and their views also will be quoted.

Although we could debate these questions all night without arriving at a conclusion, we can agree that the questions are the important ones to raise. Thus we close the first part of the service agreeing to disagree: we disagree about the answers, but we agree that the questions themselves are important and well worth asking. We are uncertain about the answers; we are certain about the questions.

Part Two

Personal Uncertainty

In this part of the service there are two modern folksongs, a poem, and a revue sketch: linked together by some of the various answers which members of the congregation wrote recently in reply to the question, "What are the things which sometimes worry you?"

The aim in this part of the service is to explore an area where there is already amongst us a considerable degree of agreement: there are many aspects of the modern world, and of our everyday lives, that make for uncertainty.

First, the song *Blowing in the Wind*, which seems to refer to various causes of worry and uncertainty in the world at large: war, disease, lack of freedom, racialism, apathy. "How many times must the cannon balls fly? . . . How many times can a man turn his head? . . ."

1. War. The future of the world.
2. Nuclear war. The destiny of the world.
3. The threat of war. The thought of the future.
4. The character and trends of modern man.
5. I am terrified by man, his readiness to hurt and kill is bad enough, but what is worse is the terrible apathy of millions.
6. The spread of disease in the world, and man's limited ability to overcome it.
7. *I* worry about my own personal problems.—Why should I worry about world affairs or the Bomb, which I can't influence by myself, is quite beyond me. If other people kill themselves, so long as they're not friends or relatives, I couldn't really care less.

Then, the poem *Undivided Loyalty*, by James Kirkup, the reaction of an individual against the claims and ideals of the larger world. "Some people would rather be dead than Red," he says, "but I would rather not be dead." And: "Jesus was wrong. . . . Nothing is worth dying for."

1. It's the thought of dying which worries me, which makes me feel lonely.
2. It's not having anything useful to do. The mods and rockers at Clacton are bored and frustrated, and so am I.
3. I worry about the way I don't think to any purpose on occasions, and about my cynicism.
4. I worry if things go wrong for my friends. Or do I? Maybe I even like it, deep down.
5. I worry about being lonely. The purpose of life is to love and be loved. I pray that someone some day will return to me the love I feel for other people. I also worry because I cannot always be myself with other people—if only people knew how I lie, and act out someone else's life.
6. It's the inability to communicate which alarms me most. Life, especially at Clifton, is so geared that self-interest and self-advancement are the dominant themes. It's surely horrifying, the total lack of intention, the total lack of attempt, at communication with other people.

7. I'm hoping I don't starve to death. I'm hoping I don't die of cancer either. I'm hoping I don't die.

Third, the revue sketch, *That's Your Trouble*, by Harold Pinter. The author draws attention to, and makes us laugh at, the way in which people often spend more time trying to impress each other than trying really to talk to, and listen to, each other. Here, two men meet by chance in a park and have a conversation about a third man: neither is the remotest bit interested in the third man as a human being, each is just out to impress and dominate the other.

In the modern world, and especially in the life of a place such as Clifton, there seems to be a continual need to "put up a façade"—to be "successful" or "amusing" or "co-operative", and people have the feeling that their real, genuine selves underneath are not being expressed—and that they are not making contact with the real, genuine selves of others. You fill in an application form, for a job or for a place at university, and give all the details about yourself: your "A" levels, your positions of responsibility, your games, your interests. These are the "details" which are measurable, the details which others can see and judge you by, these are "your image". And it can be a worry—the knowledge that there is more to the individual personality than all these things: but *what* exactly?

1. My public image. I could be shut away from the world and, if I weren't lonely, I'd be satisfied. I find that I'm often trying to make the best and show the best of myself with other people, instead of being myself. I reach the stage of not knowing who or what I am.
2. What worries me is the feeling of being caught between two realities which don't connect. On the one hand, the outer life worries—my image to others, my ambition, my work, my sexual desires. On the other, an unknown mass of feeling inside me which only sometimes surfaces and frightens me.
3. What other people think of me—especially girls—worries me. And whether or not I can play the fool and amuse everyone and still be taken seriously when I try to be serious.

4. I am moulding my outward characteristics to be a success. This is obviously necessary, but I worry that I am totally losing my real self.
5. The things that worry me a lot I keep to myself, unwilling to admit their existence. I try to ignore them, putting up a façade of humour. Nothing worries him, they say, he's always laughing. This increases the feeling that no-one understands. Do I want anyone to understand, though? My ability to mystify people is the only thing I have. But how alone it makes you feel.

Part Two of the service closes with the modern folksong *All my Trials*, a song about doubt and worry and uncertainty, but which expresses also, and more especially, a positive belief and certainty that things will turn out all right. It is "optimism in the midst of uncertainty". The song recalls, to some extent, the note on which Part One of the service ended. We are uncertain about the answers concerning religion, but certain that the questions are important: we have apparently insoluble worries in our everyday lives but are nevertheless certain that it is better to face these worries, knowing that they are shared, than to pretend that they are not there.

Part Three

Uncertainty and Certainty

In this, final part of the service the emphasis is on certainty as well as on uncertainty. There are three items: two pieces of organ music, and an extract from a Christian sermon. Both of the composers, and the preacher, have a deep faith that life is worth living, that life has some point. But theirs is not an optimism that is glib or blind: or unaware of the very good case against itself.

First, a chorale prelude by Bach: *Wir glauben all' an einen Gott*, based on a metrical form of the creed which used to be sung by the Lutheran Church. "We all believe in one God" is the subject, and also the inspiration, of the piece. Bach lived at a time when there was, at any rate in comparison with our own time, a great deal of deep certainty, when there was a generally-held view that "man is made for the vision of God". Here is a statement of that faith, the recurring, striding theme on the pedals an expression of Bach's joy and confidence—and of his certainty.

Then, a part of the sermon *Born in the Grave* by the American preacher and philosopher, Paul Tillich, whose lifelong work has been the search for new ways of expressing what he considers to be the fundamental truths about man. His belief—his optimism—is not at all an "easy answer" to all the questions of life, it is not just a "happy ending". Rather, as Tillich insists in this passage, it is only in the depths of doubt and misery that real certainty can be born.

Finally, *Dieu parmi nous* by Olivier Messiaen. Contrary (perhaps) to first appearances, this piece—it is a meditation on the birth of Christ—is as confident and as joyful as the chorale prelude by Bach, and it is meticulously ordered. The difference lies partly in the comparatively new musical techniques which Messiaen uses, but primarily in the fact that this is music which, like Tillich's sermon, is of our time. Its optimism, the certainty which it expresses, is not an "easy answer", but arrived at with full knowledge of doubt and of uncertainty. The opening three loud measures express the idea of God coming to earth, the following soft measures the idea of peace on earth, and the remaining part is an expression of joy.

Some controversy:

> The domain of morals (is) as chartless as the sea once was, and as treacherous as the sea still is. It is not too much to say that whoever wishes to become a truly moral human being (and let us not ask whether ot not this is possible: I think that we must *believe* that it is possible) must first divorce himself from all the prohibitions, crimes, and hypocrisies of the Christian church. If the concept of God has any validity at all, it can only be to make us larger, freer, and more loving. If God cannot do this, then it is time we got rid of Him.'
>
> James Baldwin, *The Fire Next Time*

> Every day on the radio, in the press and on television, the Church hawks around its Jesus figure like a vacuum cleaner, but nobody feels inclined to buy a machine that not only fails to beat, sweep or clean,

but actually makes a nice mess as well. It has *Jesus* written on the bag, but the bag contains only the air of another bunch of overpaid liars. When the Jesus jingles come on, most people simply switch off their responses automatically, and wait for the next programme. They know that the people selling the product are themselves utterly incapable of making the damned thing *work*. They behave exactly like the people who are selling something else, or who, better still, aren't selling anything at all.

. . . During the past fifty years the Church has repeatedly ducked every moral issue that has been thrown at its head—poverty, unemployment, fascism, war, South Africa, the H Bomb, and so on. It has lived in an atmosphere of calm casual funk . . .

John Osborne, *Declaration*

A virtuous man can almost cease to believe in Hell, but he carried Hell about with him. Sometimes at night he dreamed of it. . . . Evil ran like malaria in his veins. He remembered a dream he had had of a big grassy arena lined with the statues of the saints—but the saints were alive, they turned their eyes this way and that, waiting for something. He waited, too, with an awful expectancy: bearded Peters and Pauls, with Bibles pressed to their breasts, watched some entrance behind his back he couldn't see—it had the menace of a beast. Then a marimba began to play, tinkly and repetitive, a firework exploded, and Christ danced into the arena—danced and postured with a bleeding painted face, up and down, up and down, grimacing like a prostitute, smiling and suggestive. He woke with the sense of complete despair that a man might feel finding the only money he possessed was counterfeit.

Graham Greene, *The Power and the Glory*

In the more distant past, even if parental affection was lacking, working-class children grew up in a community which had strong views on right and wrong: this morality perhaps owed more to the solidarity of a group who had shared rough times than to the formal Christian ethics in which the better-class children were instructed. Today, however, both the popular and the churchgoing types of morality have tended to slip into disuse. Popular morality is now a waste land, littered with the debris of broken convictions. Concepts such as honour or even honesty, have an old-fashioned sound; but nothing has taken their place.

Professor Carstairs, *This Island Now*

I want to suggest that because England is stifling in the fumes of an emerging secular-humanist ethic, her voice is unlikely to be heard effectively when major moral issues (such as *apartheid*) are being debated in the world forum.

This ethic will always avoid what is hard and choose the soft option. It cannot do otherwise, for it is based solely on a pragmatic view of human behaviour. Man in himself and for himself is alone worth consideration. Society must be ordered, not to any ultimate good, but to a present, immediate comfort and satisfaction. And because the human passions clamour so, let them be pacified. . . .

(Christians) . . . know, and rejoice in knowing, that the conflicts and tensions, the joys and sorrows, which are part of our human condition here, are not meaningless, disconnected experiences, but are the very stuff of Love. And amongst them the needs for self-discipline and restraint are recognizably of supreme importance. Without them, love can degenerate into lust; affection into selfishness; surrender into defeat.

The artist has his vision and it is obscured by a failure in discipline. The musician, too, has his vision, and it is muffled by a refusal of discipline.

Man is made for the vision of God—that is all that he *is* made for.

Bishop Trevor Huddleston, *The Observer*, Jan. 3, 1965

A SERVICE FOR THOSE LEAVING SCHOOL

(used at Greenwich and Gravesend)

Hymn.

Reader: We are about to leave school for the wider world:
Therefore we come together to welcome new freedoms,
to give thanks for our heritage,
to face the world that awaits us,
to set out in the faith of the perfect Man, Jesus Christ.
And we are met in the presence of God our Father, who made us,
in the fellowship of Christ our Brother, who saves us,
in the power of God the invisible spirit, who inspires us.

(*all sit*)

WE WELCOME NEW FREEDOMS:

Reader: The routines of our former life are passing away now.
We have outgrown the formal relationships that have protected and disciplined us.
We leave behind the shelter of the school,
And there will be a decided difference at home.
The strong regulation of school's communal life is over,
And we enter the arena of a free society.

Prayer.

Reader: Lord, it is your will for us to welcome new freedoms,
We welcome new freedom to embark on a career,
freedom to earn our own money, or to train to earn it,
freedom to spend our money or to save it,
freedom to fashion new routines and to plan leisure,
freedom to bear new responsibilities,
freedom to make fresh meaning out of life.
We welcome new freedom to grow into the world you have given us,
to travel to the destination you have prepared for us,
to meet and serve the people you have waiting for us.

Reader:	*Leavers:*
In the challenge of freedom,	Equip us.
In the decisions of freedom,	Direct us.
In the art of freedom,	Discipline us.
In the dangers of freedom,	Protect us.
In the raptures of freedom,	Steady us.
In the life of freedom,	Give us joy.
In the use of freedom,	Grant us wisdom and the long view.
Lord, hear our prayer.	And help us to use these new freedoms responsibly.

Reader: In the factory, or firm, in college or office,
In hospital or prison, in city or on the land,
In coffee bar or on the motor way,
In whatever place, in whatever condition,

Leavers: We are always free to love our neighbour,
We are always free to love our God.

Reader: There need not be jealousy or strife between the generations.
Let us know comradeship with those who are older
And comradeship with those who will come after us,
Seeing that we share the same world, and head for the same destination.

Leavers: Help us to love in the spirit of Christ.

Hymn.

Reading: John 16: 25–33.

TO FACE THE WORLD THAT AWAITS US:

Reader: We are in the same world, and we shall have trouble.
We are in the same boat, and the boat is being rocked.
We are of the same population, and the population is exploding.
We are on the same road, and the road is blocked.
What a world! twenty-one million people killed in one war and the wars still go on.
Everyone still at a loss to know how to turn enemies into friends,
and win their way of life without threat of nuclear disaster.
Two-thirds of the world kept hungry.
Over one hundred killed every week on British roads.

Leavers: Now it is our turn to join in.
We shall be responsible too.

PRAYER FOR PROTECTION:

Reader: To bear this responsibility we shall need your protection, Lord—the armour-plating of your spirit.

Leavers: O Lord, protect us.

Reader: Protect us from the big business men who see us as industrial fodder.

Leavers: Yes, Lord protect us. (*This response is continued after each sentence of the Reader.*)

Reader: From the slick salesmen who treat us as easy market for industrial and commercial trash,

From the glib advertisements that promise success for the price of a tube of toothpaste or a bottle of deodorant,

From the pressure of unscrupulous competition, from the status symbol, and the hankering lust for money, position and power,

From those who would foul our minds, soil our bodies, and ignore our spirits,

From the world, the bomb, the drug, and the road crash,

From ourselves—for we are often our worst enemy. We are like hit and run drivers; we injure our personalities by the speed with which we move on the surface, rushing on, leaving our injured and dying spirits alone.

WE SET OUT IN THE FAITH OF THE PERFECT MAN:

Reading: John 8: 31–6 ending with: "If the Son sets you free, you will indeed be free."

Reader 1: What, free to suffer?

Reader 2: Yes, but to bear it, and to make meaning out of it.

Reader 1: What, free to stand the relentless din and monotony of the factory?

Reader 2: Yes, but not to be dehumanized by it.

Reader 1: What, free to take interminable exams?

Reader 2: Yes, but not to be victimized by them.

Reader 1: What, free to be involved in the sins of mankind?

Reader 2: Yes, but to be forgiven by the One upon whom they fall.

Reader 1: What, free to believe in a God of love in a world of ruin?

Reader 2: Yes, but not without proving Him to be true.

Reader 1: What, free to die?

Reader 2: Yes, but only to find you are sons and daughters of God and meant for eternity.

Readers 1 *and* 2: Against all the victimization of the world
Jesus has set us free
And we are free indeed!

Reader 2: So in the freedom of the Son, the perfect Man,
We shall make money honestly,
We shall make love honourably,
We shall make time for those who need us,
We shall make friends of our enemies,
We shall make amends straightaway,
We shall make Him supreme,
For His service in the world is perfect freedom.

Hymn.
Address.
Hymn.
Blessing.

A SERVICE FOR GOOD FRIDAY EVENING

(used at Clapham, Good Friday 1967)

Theme of service: the meaning of life and death as seen through the Cross

a. Facing life—the costliness of love;
b. Facing death—the triumph of love.

FACING LIFE AND ITS MEANING

The conductor of the service opens with:

First let us sing the hymn: "Fill thou my life, O Lord my God,
In every part with praise."

As you were singing that hymn did that reflect your own attitude to life? Is that what life means to you? If you were asked tomorrow, "What is the meaning of your life?" would you know how to answer?

There are many answers that have been given and are being given now. Let us hear some of them.

Reader 1: For some, life has no meaning at all. Hear the words of the great writer, Albert Camus: "Life has no meaning. To live is to make the absurd live. To make it live is to face it squarely. The important thing is not to live better but to live more."

Reader 2: For some, life means just loneliness: listen to that great song of the Beatles which is a classic account in words and music of the theme of loneliness. (*Eleanor Rigby*.)

Reader 3: For some, life is something from which to seek escape. Listen to the testimony of a drug addict as to why he takes drugs: "I take them to escape from the monotony of the real world into the world of my dreams so that for a while I can be free of the inhibitions of ordinary life and live in a world where I can feel and experience what ordinary life never gives me."

Reader 4: For some, life is a struggle for freedom from the bondages and prejudices of society. Listen to the stirring song of the Freedom marchers of America. (*We shall overcome*.)

Reader 5: For some, life is money, pleasure, power or the building of a new world. A boy of 15 in a modern psalm speaks of this and yet of the realization that this is not all of life. (Quote from *Psalm* in *Modern Psalms of Boys*, on page 93 of this book.)

Conductor: All of us sometimes feel a sense of frustration about life—the spirit of this is well caught by Michel Quoist in one of his *Prayers of Life*'. (Here quote from the Prayer, *Lord deliver me from myself* from the words, "Alone, I am bored" to the words "I hurt myself.") But in that same prayer Christ answers him with the words,

"Why choose to be a prisoner of yourself?
You are free."

What does the Cross tell us of that freedom? Let both the hymn which we are to sing and the address which is to follow help us with the answer.

Hymn: *Most Glorious Lord of Life*.

Address: on the Cross as the meaning of life. The meaning of life is love because the meaning of God is love, but love is costly and the freedom of "we shall overcome" is only found when the costliness is faced. (This is to be basically the theme of the address.)

FACING DEATH AND ITS MEANING

The conductor opens the second half of the service with the words:

But there is another side to the Cross of Christ. If there is shown the meaning of life, there also is shown the meaning and the facing of death. Here, as with the meaning of life, there are many answers given as to the meaning of death. Let us hear some of them:

Reader 1: For many today, death is death without God: Death is not to be mentioned or spoken of. Men fear death and would put it away from their thinking. An article in *The Observer* in March 1967, spoke of this: "Death is as untouchable a subject, as was sex in Victorian England. Taboo or not taboo? Are people scared of the dying and the dead? Having apparently become less confident of what follows death, they may be less willing than previous generations to confront it. In the course of research for this article most people when asked if they had thought about death said: 'I find death, with or without God, too disturbing to contemplate voluntarily'."

Reader 2: For many, death spells the pointlessness of life: Hear the words of two humanists: "Life leads to nothing and every pretence that it does not is a deceit. If there is a bridge over a gorge which spans only half the distance and ends in mid-air, and if the bridge is crowded with human beings pressing on, one after another they fall into the abyss. The bridge leads nowhere, and those who are pressing forward to cross it are going nowhere." H. J. Blackham *Objections to Humanism:* page 119), or Bertrand Russell: "No fire, no heroism, no intensity of thought or feeling can preserve an individual life beyond the grave."

Reader 3: For many, death is regarded wistfully as simply the end of the trials of life. Listen to this view of death sung most beautifully by Joan Baez (*All my Trials* by Joan Baez).

Reader 4: The common feelings of the ordinary man about death are well expressed at the beginning of one of Michel Quoist's poems (The first two stanzas of *The Funeral*).

Conductor: But none of these is the way Christ looks at death as

He faces it upon the Cross: (Here follows address on the meaning of death as revealed through the Cross in which basically the theme is that life is through death and not in spite of death, that every decision of life is a decision for life or death eternally, that death is to be faced, not avoided; but that if love is the meaning of life, then love which is creative has power over the destructive which is death).

CONCLUSION

Conductor: Life through death, death through life—these are the great realities of human living revealed through the Cross. Let us then end with the resolve expressed through one of Quoist's prayers, saying after me:

> "Lord, help me to travel along my road faithfully at my proper place in the vast procession of humanity, for it would be a lie to weep before your lifeless image, if I did not follow you, living, on the road that men travel."

And in that resolve, let us find reassurance for life and for death in the words of St. Paul and in one of our own great Easter hymns:

Reading: Romans 8: 34 to end.

Hymn: *Love's redeeming work is done.*

USEFUL BOOKS FOR THE FURTHER STUDY OF CONTEMPORARY SPIRITUALITY

BOOKS OF PRAYERS IN CONTEMPORARY LANGUAGE AND SITUATIONS:

MALCOLM BOYD, *Are you running with me, Jesus?* (Holt, Rinehart and Winston, New York).

ROBERT CASTLE, *Litany of the Ghetto* (reproduced in *New Christian*, June 2, 1966)

LOUIS EVELY, *That man is you* (Newman Press, Westminster, Maryland, U.S.A.)

BRIAN FROST, *Reflections for the Urban Man* (about to be published).

RAYMOND HEARN, *Modern Psalms by Boys* (University of London Press Ltd).

CHIARA LUBICH, *The Christian Eye* (New City Press, New York) (founder of the Focolare Movement).

WILLIAM OPEL, *Seeing and Praying* (reproduced in *New Christian*, Sept. 8, 1966).

MICHEL QUOIST, *Prayers of Life* (Gill & Son, Dublin).

ROBERT RAINES, *Creative Brooding* (Macmillan Co., New York).

New Hymns for a New Day (published by World Council of Churches, obtainable from British Council of Churches, 10 Eaton Gate, S.W.1).

BOOKS ON PRAYER VALUABLE TO AN UNDERSTANDING OF CONTEMPORARY SPIRITUALITY:

LOUIS BOUYER, *Introduction to Spirituality* (Darton, Longman and Todd Ltd., London).

EUGENE BOYLAN, *Difficulties in Mental Prayer* (Gill and Son Ltd., Dublin).

B. C. BUTLER, *Prayer, an adventure in living* (Darton, Longman and Todd, London).

PAMELA CARSWELL, *Offbeat Spirituality* (Sheed and Ward Ltd., London).

PIERRE CHARLES, S.J., *Prayer for All Times* (Sands and Co., London).

LOUIS EVELY, *We Dare to Say Our Father* (Herder and Herder: New York).
GEORGE MACLEOD: *Only One Way Left*, Chapter 8 (Iona Community).
MAURICE NEDONCELLE, *The Nature and the Use of Prayer* (Burns & Oates, London).
D. Z. PHILLIPS, *The Concept of Prayer* (Routledge and Kegan Paul, London).
ROGER SCHUTZ, PRIOR OF TAIZE, *Living Today for God* and *This Day Belongs to God* (Helicon Press, Maryland, U.S.A. and Faith Press, London).
TEILHARD DE CHARDIN, *Le Milieu Divin* and *Hymn of the Universe* (Collins, London).
MARTIN THORNTON, *Christian Proficiency* (S.P.C.K., London).

CLASSICAL BOOKS VALUABLE TO AN UNDERSTANDING OF CONTEMPORARY SPIRITUALIRY:

WALTER HILTON, *The Scale of Perfection* (Burns Oates, London).
JULIAN OF NORWICH, *Revelations of Divine Love* (Burns Oates, London).
The Cloud of Unknowing, (Burns Oates).
St Teresa, Complete Works, ed. Alison-Peers (Sheed and Ward).
St John of the Cross, Complete Works (Newman).

FOR UNDERSTANDING OF LITURGY:

BISHOP OF WOOLWICH, *Liturgy Coming to Life* (S.C.M. PRESS).
BISHOP OF WOOLWICH, *Honest to God* (chapter 5), (S.C.M. Press).
H. WILSON, *Living the Liturgy Together* (Church Information Office).
R. LAMBOURNE, *Church, Community and Healing* (Darton, Longman & Todd).

VALUABLE PERIODICALS:

The Way: A Quarterly Review of Christian Spirituality (published by Society of Jesus, Farm St., London).
Concilium: Spirituality (November 1965), (Burns Oates).
Worship: A journal published by the Benedictines at The Liturgical Press, Minnesota and obtainable through Duckett, London).